Dream Floors

Dream Floors

Hundreds of Design Ideas
for Every Kind of Floor

KATHLEEN STOEHR

RANDALL

RANDALL INTERNATIONAL

Published in the United States by:
Randall International
San Clemente, California

Distributed in Great Britain by:
Antique Collectors Club Ltd
Woodbridge, Suffolk

Second Edition

ISBN 1-890379-11-5

www.randallonline.com
Editor-in-Chief: Kathleen M. Stoehr
Book Interior: Chemistry Creative, Minneapolis, MN
Photo Research: Kathleen M. Stoehr
Cover Design: Diego Linares
Cover Credits: Cover: Capella Wood Floors; Inside Front: Kirkstone; Title page: Integraf; This Page & Contents: Oceanside Glasstile; Back cover: Amtico International; Capella Wood Floors; Nourison USA. *Please refer to the Source Guide for additional information.*

10987654321

Library of Congress Cataloging-in-Publication Data
Stoehr, Kathleen, 1960-
Dream floors : hundreds of design ideas for every kind of floor / by
Kathleen S. Stoehr.-- 2nd ed.
p. cm.
Includes bibliographical references and index.
ISBN 1-890379-11-5 (pbk.)
1. Flooring. 2. Floors. I. Title.

TH2521.S7854 2005b
721'.6--dc22
2005030687

CONTENTS

Introduction	6
Question Yourself	8–9
The Caveats	11
Radiant Heat	13
Hardwood	14–55
Carpet & Rugs	56–87
Resilient	88–127
Laminate	128–157
Tile & Stone	158–209
Alternative Floor Coverings	210–221
Glossary of Terms	223–232
Source Guide	233–236
Index	237–239
Resources	240

INTRODUCTION

Step Away from that Flat Screen!

AS WITH JUST ABOUT ANY PURCHASE, there are a number of mostly predictable steps involved in moving from initial enthusiasm about a new item to actual purchase of said item. You should be able to identify many of these steps—anticipation, exploration and decision, to name a few. So, what does a new flat screen television have to do with your flooring purchase?

You are holding in your hands a flooring lifeline…because step three in the mostly predictable five step plan to buying a new floor for your home is, indeed, throwing up your hands in defeat and marching over to the closest electronics store to assuage your flooring frustration with fancy gadgets. Completely and entirely stepping away from the hardwood, the resilient, the soft loopy crush of carpet underneath your feet, and just plain forgetting you ever wanted a new floor in the first place. Because it's too difficult to figure out what you want when all you have in front of you are eight hundred twelve by twelve squares of vinyl samples (all in beige, of course), or two hundred million small pads of carpet to stand upon in the middle of a brightly lit mega-carpet-mega store.

Your lifeline is this book, because we will to show you what's out there, and better yet—how it actually looks in a home. We hope to help you figure out what type of flooring works best for you based on your needs, so you can walk into any flooring store with confidence and have a firm idea in your head of what you *don't* need to look at.

We're going to help you think clearly about your needs and desires for a new floor, and also help you to step outside your normal comfort lines and consider alternate colors, patterns, textures and styles.

Finally, this book won't preach to the choir. We know that if you have picked it up, chances are you want a new floor. So we will not use wonderfully cozy phrases about how your floor is the finishing touch, or how (shame on you!) a scuffed up floor is the equivalent of a badly worn pair of shoes paired with a new designer suit. Flowery verbiage will not help you select your new flooring; inspiring photographs and informative copy will. You want a new floor? Make the right choice. Step away from that electronics store and dive into *Dream Floors*.

Question Yourself

THERE ISN'T A SPECIAL DECODER RING that will help you decide which floor works best in which room. Technological advances and risk taking have shown that linoleum doesn't always belong in the kitchen, nor does wood only belong in an entryway. Heavens—if it weren't for risk taking and exploration, we'd still be sweeping the dirt off of our dirt floors.

You will be asked questions such as the following when you sit down with a consultant. Take the time to ponder them now, and you will be better prepared when the time comes.

Existing Floor

- What don't you like about your existing floor?

- Quick—what's your dream floor? Did any thought immediately pop into your head? Write it down and save it for later reference.

- Where is this floor located?

- What is currently on the floor? Do you think it could be removed easily?

- What are the approximate measurements of your space?

- Is there an adjacent stairway?

General Questions

- Have you given any thought to your budget?

- Do you have any idea whether the subfloor is structurally sound?

- Is this a heavily trafficked area or a seldomly-used room? Assess the room's level of activity and assign it as one of light use, moderate use or heavy use.

- Consider sound. If you are replacing carpet with hardwood, for example, will the lack of a sound buffer be bothersome?

- Who lives in your home? Children, pets, adults, elderly? How might your flooring be impacted by those who dwell in your home?

- What types of furniture will you have in the room? The rolling wheels of a desk chair? A heavy armoire?

- Are you interested in heating your floor?

Qualities Needed

- How long do you expect to keep the new flooring in place?

- Does it need to be moisture resistant?

- What types of safety issues do you have? (I.e., would it be important to have carpet to cushion a toddler's fall or are you interested in reduced leg fatigue; also consider if slip or fire resistancy is paramount.)

- Are you interested in championing "Green" design? (As in, do you want to select a floor covering constructed with environmentally responsible practices employed?)

- Does anyone in your home suffer from allergies?

Time Frame

- How quickly do you want to have your floor installed?

- Would you be able to vacate the area of the home your flooring is being installed for a period of one day? Three days? Five days?

Design Thoughts

- If your room is already decorated to your satisfaction, how will this new floor fit into that scheme?

- If you are beginning with a clean slate, what is your design style? Do you prefer a bright contemporary look? Or, a warm, traditional appearance? (Don't worry if you don't know—as you page through this book, you may discover a style that's just right for you!)

Finishes, Colors & Patterns

- Consider texture. How does a rough hewn plank floor compare to a highly glossed laminate, to an exotic Oriental rug? Different textures make different statements.

- Pattern can add interest and depth to a plainly designed room or make it appear smaller and wider. How do you feel about decorative flooring patterns? Stripes? Checks? Florals? Small tiling details?

- Color can tie together disparate elements in the room through a unifying tone, make a bold statement or soften harsh lines. What kinds of colors do you like best? How will they fulfill the needs of your design scheme?

Maintenance

- What type of stain/soil protection are you interested in?

- How often do you truly feel you will clean this floor? Daily? Weekly? Monthly?

Be truthful with yourself about maintenance issues, such as how often you believe you will sweep your floors. If you choose a flooring that is high maintenance and your style is more low maintenance, you will ultimately be disappointed with your floors' performance. *Shown:* Canadian Birch solid hardwood flooring. Typically, sweeping once a day to remove grit is the best defense.

The Caveats

There is a moral to this story.

THE SAD TRUTH ABOUT FLOORING is that it typically stays down longer than it should—usually, until someone gets tired of looking at it. Or sometimes, it's perfectly fine and yet up it comes anyway, because . . . someone is tired of looking at it. Thus, when we speak of the typical life cycle of a particular flooring material, it isn't without caveats. Animals, toddlers, high heels, cleats, chairs being dragged across a kitchen floor to reach a high cupboard. Floors take a beating. There are no hard and fast rules.

There are also caveats to be considered when looking at pricing. Prices will fluctuate dependent upon the area of the country, the venue it was purchased from and also who is installing the material. As we all know, it's important to get three bids on any project so you can gauge these fluctuations and make an educated decision.

Then there's maintenance. Be really truthful with yourself about this issue. I swore I'd vacuum my new plush broadloom frequently, because it was of the type that showed every little teeny weenie dog hair, every footprint, every piece of lint. I *had* to have that carpet. And I wasn't being truthful with myself because I abhor vacuuming, so now, more frequently than I'd like to admit, I am assailed by teeny weenie dog hairs, footprints and the like. The moral of this story: if you're not planning to take care of your flooring as suggested by the manufacturer—don't buy it! Lack of proper maintenance on any type of flooring: unswept grit that acts like sandpaper underfoot, unvacuumed carpet, for instance, can remove years and beauty from its life.

be truthful with yourself and you are less apt to be disappointed

Be sure, too, that you are very careful in your product specification. Throughout the compilation of this book, I came across more than a handful of companies that never truly stated clearly that its products were faux. A "Stone" collection, for example, may very well be glazed porcelain made to look like slate or limestone. Or it may even be resilient! Many of the products on the market today are so lovingly copied it may be hard to tell the difference. If you want real wood, real stone—be absolutely certain you are getting it. Faux products are frequently given the moniker of a real product.

Finally, when it comes to spending, buy the best floor covering you can afford. This is not the place to skimp. There is not a thing in your home that doesn't take more abuse than your floors. Be kind to them, spend freely on them, and they will provide you with years of unending beauty.

Radiant heating under ceramic tile in a bathroom area keeps toes cozy. *Shown*: Florida Tile offers Tivoli, large sized, glazed porcelain designed for architectural beauty and strength. Suble color variegation and a slight semi-matte undulation make things interesting; a combination of tile patterns makes a dramatic, yet soothing statement.

Radiant Heat

Underneath it all, radiant heating keeps you cozy.

ONE ITEM THAT WILL NOT BE DIRECTLY ADDRESSED in this book, except for this page, is the topic of radiant floor heating. While radiant heating has been around for centuries (Romans/bathhouses/heated water running in small troughs below the floors/*ahhh*), it is only recently that innovations have allowed every type of flooring on every level of the home to benefit from this bottoms-up heating luxury.

There are two types of radiant heating: hydronic (water) and electric, but each work in approximately the same manner: tubing (for water) or wire (for electric) is run underneath the subfloor. The heat radiates and is controlled by a separate thermostat, typically set at about 85 degrees. Being that heat falls, this warmth stays grounded, leaving toes believing summer is afoot, even in the snowiest of seasons.

Advantages are many. First, of course, is the exceptional savings radiant heating imparts on ones' heating bill. Though expensive to install (think approximately five dollars per square foot), it will pay for itself over the course of about six years. Second, the heating is not airborne, so you will not experience a lack of humidity due to this increased energy source. Radiant heating is also silent and does not stir up dust or other inflight particles, again, due to the fact that it is a contained heat.

radiant heating imparts exceptional savings throughout the years

There are a few things to remember. One is that you should not exceed the recommended maximum temperature as it could, for example, warp natural surfaces such as solid hardwood flooring. And, overheating will stress the radiant system.

Contractors should be involved early in the process and complete a heating load estimate to uncover where your home may have cold spots and design the system that's best for your needs. Additionally, pumped up sections of radiant can be installed to offer what is almost a "curtain" to contain heat leaks (near a window area or entryway, for example).

But don't think that radiant heating is just for the interior of a home, however. For those who embrace the cold while living in the north, radiant heating in a walkway or driveway will eliminate the need to chisel ice and snow.

Hardwood

IN A WORLD WHERE EVERYONE SEEMS TO BE MULTI-TASKING, plugged in and racing from one responsibility to the next, the timeless look of wood floors offer a haven from the internal storm. In a sense, wood brings the outside in, connecting us with nature and suggesting a warmth and beauty which only increases in value as the years pass.

There's nothing like the resonant tone of heels on hardwood; the imperfections that a nail hole or a bird beak will imbue. These marks are reassuring, comforting. And because they are such, the very nature of these unique imperfections make wood one of the most appealing of flooring materials. Available in a variety of forms: solid, engineered or reclaimed, you can rest assured that there is a wood floor to suit whatever your needs may be.

This 42" x 42" inlay of Brazilian cherry, poplar, wenge and white oak is a beautiful accent piece, inspired by a detail the designer saw in a 14th century wood and ivory inlay.

History in the Making

Wood floors have been around since the Middle Ages, rough hewn planks, formed by broad axe or hand-scraped by our forefathers; trod upon in little houses on the big prairies, to farm houses and ranches, to the most glorious of mansions. A hundred years ago, most trees destined for flooring were chopped and then floated down the river to a sawmill, which would cut the tree into random widths. Returned to the homeowner, the logs would then be hand-scraped to as smooth and even a surface as possible, and then installed. Early manufacturers in the late 1800s primarily employed oak because it was prolific, accessible and strong, but also because it performed well when interacting with newly developed equipment.

And while many throughout the twentieth century embraced wood floors, new innovations, such as resilient flooring, gave way to homeowner experimentation. Wood was covered by vinyl, carpet, linoleum. It was deemed passé, so Old World. By the 1970s, it seemed everything was covered in shag carpet or vinyl sheet.

And yet, as these newer flooring materials deteriorated and were removed, homeowners were delighted to find rich, warm wood underneath. Still viable, still beautiful. Permanent.

Left: Makeshift log rafts, sawmill bound. Photo courtesy of Goodwin Heart Pine.

Today's Wood

In today's more environmentally-conscious world, it is recognized that wood is a renewable and recyclable natural resource. And, not only is newly cut wood an option for floors, but reclaimed wood as well.

Twenty-first century technology offers over fifty domestic and exotic species of wood, with countless price ranges, colors, grades, cuts and more. Best of all, an intermittent sanding and refinishing basically results in a brand new floor.

Unique and beautiful, you can rest assured that your wood floor will be the only one of its kind—because, as different as every snowflake, that is how each board measures out. No growth ring is the same and no wormhole, bird peck or pitch pocket is ever in an identical position. Wood is inimitable, warm and best of all, comes with a lifetime guarantee. The life of the wood, that is—which is far longer than yours will *ever* be.

Below: Ebony bamboo flooring makes a strong statement in this Louisville, KY private residence.

Reclaimed Wood

If you are a recycler by heart yet love wood floors, you need look no further than reclaimed, recycled wood. Typically salvaged from old barns, railroad ties, dock pilings, fence posts and even from lumber long lost at the bottom of the drink, this guilt-free flooring option offers historic appeal matched with exceptional quality.

One reclaimed wood purveyor, for example, working closely with government officials to ensure protection of the river environment, uses state licensed diving crews to recover heart pine logs from the state's Suwannee River. Originally slated for the mill hundreds of years ago, these logs broke free of the makeshift rafts used to float them down river and finally sunk to an oxygen-free resting place. The water does little to harm the wood; in fact, it becomes so impregnated with fortifying minerals that once dry, it is even more durable than in its original state.

Another manufacturer makes use of old barn wood from nearby areas,

resanding and replaning to make some of the most sturdy, hardwearing wood floors in the U.S.

And, due to environmental restrictions (among other things), much of this wood: heart pine, redwood and chestnut, is no longer available as new flooring material. Add in the unique patinas, saw marks, wormholes and knots and you will have a one-of-a-kind, environmentally-savvy product on your floors.

Old barnwood is reclaimed and made new again. Photo courtesy of Aged Woods.

River Recovered® heart cypress select is a blend of vertical with feathery grain and is 100% heartwood. Available up to 10 inches wide, there are no nail holes.

The Facts: Reclaimed Wood

Advantages: A "cradle-to-cradle" product: once useful, it has been recycled to even greater acclaim; exceedingly strong; unique due to natural patterns and distinctive markings; soft underfoot; easy to repair with just a sanding

Disadvantages: Expensive; not as effective in areas where water, humidity and/or moisture may be a problem, such as bathrooms; can expand and contract due to fluctuations in humidity; color of the floor may change over time due to a variety of environmental effects such as sunlight, chemical introduction and more

Cost: $5–$100 per square foot, depending upon grade, type, etc.

Lifespan: Centuries

Most Appropriate Locations: Kitchens, living and dining rooms, bedrooms. Basically, any area where moisture isn't.

Care & Cleaning: Do not wet mop; only a damp mop or a mild wood cleaner is necessary. Sweep to remove dirt and other particles.

Left: The inner beauty and luster exhibited in reclaimed woods shines on flooring and a staircase bannister.

Above: Premium select vertical grain heart pine is 95% heartwood with a natural color variation. Characterized by infrequent nail holes and 80 percent knot free, it is available in standard lengths of two to 11 feet in length, with five to seven feet being average.

Heart pine was once the premier building material in the U.S.— virtually every factory or warehouse built before World War I incorporated beams of this strong, durable wood. Today, less than 1% of the original forest remains.

Dream Floors

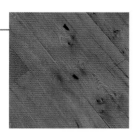

Left: American gothic white oak reclaimed wood has a beauty that goes far beyond the sense of history it harbors. Precision milled to exacting standards, it lends a relaxed look to any room.

Upper right: This private residence in North Andover, MA shows custom millwork and beautiful wood floors in antique American chestnut. Photo courtesy of Warren Jaeger Photography.

The Facts: Solid Wood

Advantages: Natural and warm; exceedingly strong; unique due to natural patterns and distinctive markings; soft underfoot; easy to repair with just a sanding; glueless technology allows for installation below grade

Disadvantages: Dust from exotic wood (when being refurbished or installed) can prompt allergies that might not be provoked by domestic woods such as oak or maple; not as effective in areas where water, humidity and/or moisture may be a problem, such as bathrooms; can expand and contract due to fluctuations in humidity; color may change over time due to a variety of environmental effects such as sunlight, chemical introduction and more

Cost: Costs will vary dependant upon the type and grade of wood selected, but in general, costs will range from $2.50 to $50 per square foot

Lifespan: Centuries

Most Appropriate Locations: Kitchens, living and dining rooms, bedrooms. Basically, any area where moisture isn't.

Care & Cleaning: Do not wet mop; only a damp mop or a mild wood cleaner is necessary. Sweep to remove dirt and other particles.

Left: Pecan plank candle glow-toned engineered wood flooring creates a warm, sensuous environment.

Upper right: Alpine ash classic starts as a tall tree found in the cooler high altitudes of the Australian Alps, and ends as a lovely creamy light floor with excellent dimensional stability.

Lower right: Sleek and clean, hardwood flooring is a beautiful accent to the wood cabinetry and window blinds.

Hardwood

Good to Know: Your Wood Floor

There are over fifty species of wood currently used in flooring, from reclaimed wood to newly harvested to engineered to exotics. How do you take care of these beautiful, natural products? What does refinishing entail? What's the best floor for your situation? Here are some points to ponder:

- **Consider Acrylic Impregnated:** Acrylic is forced into the pores of the wood, providing it with a built-in "wear system" which allows less maintenance and greater durability. Use in a high traffic location.

- **Consider Bamboo:** The Moso species of bamboo is harvested when it reaches about ninety feet high and eight to twelve feet in diameter. While it looks like a tree, acts like a tree and makes dandy flooring, it's actually . . . grass. Fast growing, it is not the type of bamboo used for feeding animals, thus it is not depleting a potential food group. Its root systems also help it regrow after harvest. As solid as hard maple and much more stable than red oak, bamboo offers high quality along with exceptional durability.

- **Consider Safety:** Never use a self-polishing acrylic wax on a wood floor, as it will cause extreme slickness. Additionally, that high polish you just achieved will become dull quickly.

- **Consider Time Frames:** Refinishing a floor is not a quick, simple task. Plenty of time is involved in not only the sanding, but the removal of any kind of contaminent, such as dust or grit (which will—Murphy's Law!—typically not show up until after the second coat of finish). You should also to allow adequate time to dry not just the surface but all areas, such as cracks and corners. Remember, wood is an investment, a natural beauty—and must be treated as such.

- **Consider Radiant Heating:** Oak, ash and merbau are considered a top choice for covering in-floor radiant systems. Maple and pecan are less desirable choices.

- **Consider a Pre-finished Floor:** Prefinished at the factory, a hardwood floor will feature three to seven layers of a UV-cured polyurethane. This will provide a luxurious but tough, durable surface. Do not damp mop—in general, wood and water do not mix. Pre-finishing also eliminates many of the negatives involved in installing the floor—things such as dust from sanding and odors from the application of finishes. Time of installation is shortened as well—by up to half.

Virginia vintage walnut flooring is hand-scraped, offering rich hues and deep tones.
The dark walnut tone is the perfect foil to the whitewashed antique casegoods.

Above: Each floorboard in this living area is hand-crafted to resemble antique flooring. No two boards are identical.

- **Consider Floating Floors:** If you do not want to go through the mess of removing an existing floor, such as vinyl or ceramic, and/or rebuilding a subfloor, consider installing a floating floor, in which the wood flooring material is installed without the use of nails or adhesive, over the top of an existing floor.
- **Consider Mixed Media:** Besides the ever growing and popular inlay wood flooring accents, consider mixing tile, leather or metal into the equation. A tile border at the wall's edge, for example, will set off the interior and provide punctuation to an already beautiful material.
- **Consider Parquet Flooring:** Small pieces of wood are carefully pieced together to create beautiful patterns. Once made up of individually laid pieces in older homes, parquet is now available in six to twelve inch tiles. Be aware, however, that an extra sturdy subfloor—as well as underlayment—is needed, as parquet is non-structural.

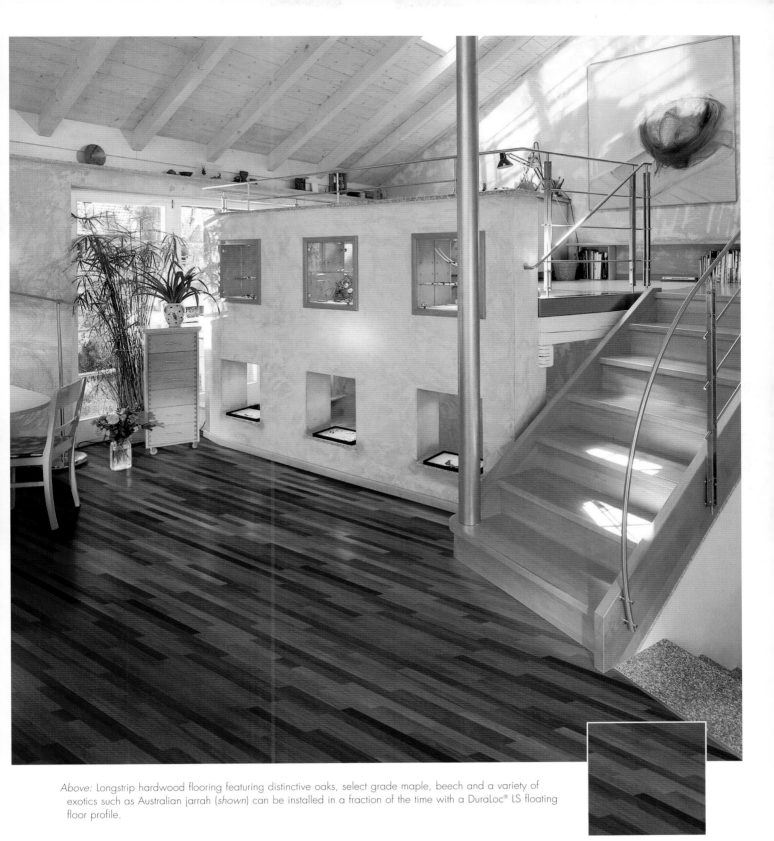

Above: Longstrip hardwood flooring featuring distinctive oaks, select grade maple, beech and a variety of exotics such as Australian jarrah (*shown*) can be installed in a fraction of the time with a DuraLoc® LS floating floor profile.

River reclaimed heart pine is imbued with color variations born from the various mineral contents of the rivers they are claimed from.

Good to Know: Grade & Cut

- **Grade**: The term "grade" refers only to the wood's appearance. There are six grades: Clear, which is considered free of defects, though it may have minor imperfections. Select, which is one step down from clear and may have some color variation and knots. The Common grade—split into Common 1 (variegated appearance) and Common 2 (rustic appearance)—is often chosen because of its natural characteristics such as knots and wormholes. First grade, which offers natural color differences and few character marks; Second, which is considered multicolored in appearance; and finally Third, which is rustic and allows all of the wood characteristics of that particular species to show.

Left: White bamboo flooring is sleek and modern in this Cleveland, OH residence.

Three and one-quarter inch Canadian maple plank flooring displays beautiful color variations to draw the eye and warm the heart.

- **Cut**: There are three different ways a board can be cut: Plainsawn, Quartersawn and Riftsawn. The most common cut is Plainsawn, which displays the grain patterns and growth rings most, as each cut is made parallel to the next. Quartersawn is more expensive, as it turns out less board feet per log, but the advantage is that this board wears more evenly due to less twisting and cupping of the wood. The log is cut into quarters and then cut perpendicular to the growth rings. Riftsawn wood is cut approximately the same way as quartersawn, but at a slightly different angle to reduce flaking. It is the most expensive of the cuts, due to the waste.

Right: Pacific bamboo flooring is harder than classic red oak and more stable than maple—a durable and innovative option.

The Facts: Engineered Wood

Advantages: Layered construction reduces the twisting and cupping that may occur in solid wood planks and strips; the most beautiful wood is used only in the top layer, allowing more efficient use of the whole tree; acclimation process is less time consuming, meaning less time for installation as well; can be installed below grade; handles changes in temperature and humidity more easily than solid wood.

Disadvantages: It isn't solid and repeated sanding and refinishing may work itself through the premium wood layer and into grades that are not as beautiful. Plus, being each layer is set at a 90 degree angle from the previous, there is possibility of grain mismatch after repeated refinishing.

Cost: Less expensive than solid wood, as premium wood is used only in the top layer. Approximately $2.50 to $50 per square foot.

Lifespan: Centuries

Most Appropriate Locations: Kitchens, living and dining rooms, bedrooms. Engineered flooring can take a little moisture, compared to solid wood flooring.

Care & Cleaning: Do not wet mop; only a damp mop or a mild wood cleaner is necessary. Sweep to remove dirt and other particles.

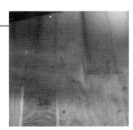

Left: Classic pecan flooring imparts a naturally distressed look with plank widths available in either 3¼" or 4½". Grain variations and knots make this a standout floor for a rustic kitchen.

Above: Inlay flooring creates a focal point in this entryway area. Consider using inlay when you want to define a space, carry a design motif from one area of your home to the next, or simply to reflect your own personal style. This particular composition includes yellow-heart, ipe, lacewood and a brass accent ring.

Dream Floors

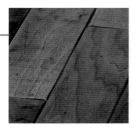

Left: Wide, handcrafted planks emphasize details of grain patterns and intricate textures.

Upper right: Most of the raw materials seen in this billiard room werere retrieved from agricultural out-buildings, e.g. barns, ranging in age from 75 years to as much as 200 years. Some of these planks are from the trees of the virgin forests, those that were alive when our ancestors arrived. Having grown during a period of unique ecological balance, this wood has a tighter grain.

Lower right: Premium wood products are beautiful when coupled with natural stone and wrought iron.

1

2

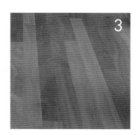
3

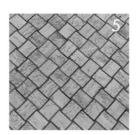
4

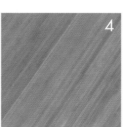
5

2

3

1: Brazilian cherry flooring is specially designed to enhance cherry's tight-grained appearance. The floor will darken to a deeper red as it ages.
2: Concentric circles of maple and oak descend to a 21", eight-pointed star of Brazilian cherry and maple. 3: Karri, native to the southwest corner of western Australia, is a lively red wood with pale pink to reddish brown overtones. 4: Six foot by six foot wide plank flooring is sleek and beautiful in this Bainbridge Island, WA residence. Photo courtesy of Teragren LLC. 5: This tearoom floor includes approximately 48 square feet of machine-cut Finnish birch and American walnut.

4

5

Exotic wood species, such as Asian beech, offers rich, luxurious color.

This teak flooring is beautifully veneered for connoisseurs of rare special types of wood (all FSC certified), a unique experience for the real wood lover.

Above: Rescued oak flooring provides a true hardwood option with plenty of character in random widths from three to seven inches.

Right: Site finished and solid, this flooring is a beautiful, natural and environmentally sustainable product. Note the changes in wood tone—a truly unique look.

Dream Floors

Left: The beauty of age-crafted engineered cherry floors shines through. This hand-hewn floor, three-quarter inch thick and with a ⅛" wear layer, offers planks five inches wide—truly exceptional.

Above: This innovative engineered hardwood flooring is available in ⅜" and ¾" thicknesses and features a ⅛" or ⅙" wear layer, respectively. A special engineering process helps resist expansion and contraction. Photo by David Lyles.

Above: Parquet flooring in maple and American cherry is set off by a detailed border.

Left: This drawing room installation uses approximately 693 square feet of machine-cut Finnish birch, American walnut, wenge, plane-tree and quartersawn oak.

Above: Engineered for superior strength and stability, the five-ply, three-quarter inch construction in this pecan flooring material virtually elimates gapping, cupping and twisting. Better yet, it can be installed on, above or below grade.

Right: Premium teak has been employed to beautiful use in this three strip installation.

Hardwood

Left: Wideplank maple premium originating from the northern part of the U.S. exhibits a unique light color and fine grain that will brighten up any home.

Upper right: The Moso species of bamboo is reincarnated as warm caramelized vertical grain flooring. This product has been manufactured to stringent, environmentally-conscious specifications. Photo by Steven Young and courtesy of Teragren LLC.

Lower right: This strip engineered flooring is available in seven finishes, including English walnut (*shown above*) and has a sliced cut, which offers a more natural, close grain appearance.

Dream Floors

Above Left: Naturally beautiful, this walnut engineered flooring is not only manufactured entirely in the United States for quicker deliveries but is also manufactured with the efficient use of raw materials, making it environmentally friendly.

Lower left: This master bedroom installation won the 2003 Best Residential Installation from the National Wood Flooring Association. It is a 650 square foot combination of Brazilian satinwood, bloodwood and maple.

Above: A distinctive "worn" look is accomplished by using distressed planks with an eased edge, as well as a unique French bleed coloring technique.

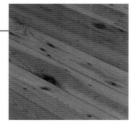

This floor is constructed of reclaimed heart pine. The bar top is from a river recovered long leaf pine log, which harbors age rings exceeding 300 years.

This lovely inlay medallion features the diverse characteristics of heart cypress and wild black cherry in addition to a variety of other hardwoods used to accentuate the colors displayed in the wood.

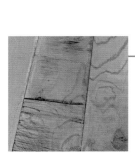

Each five inch plank is hand-scraped by skilled artisans so that no two boards are alike—absolutely stunning!

Above: Engineered wood flooring is shown in a spice oak coloration. Five other colors are available, all in a choice of two plank widths.

Above Right: Australian beech thrives in the warm and relatively humid stretch of the new South Wales coastline in high quality open forest. This strong and versatile wood is shown in its attractive cream to pale brown coloration.

Lower Right: Winner of the 2002 Best Use of Wood Technology Floor of the Year, awarded by the National Wood Flooring Association, this floor combines classic design and contemporary flair in this high-end parquet floor. Combining quartersawn oak and Karelian birch for the main area of the floor with American walnut, Austrian pear and Karelian birch for the outside border, the floor was finished by spraying on two coats of sealer and five coats of waterbased finish. Taking 90 days to complete, this floor was a lengthy process, but well deserved for its beauty.

Above: This solid, elegant birch hardwood floor is factory finished for exceptional color and fast, easy installation.

Left: Premium five inch character pecan plank is engineered for installation at any level of the home and also offers coordinated transition pieces for thresholds, stairways and more.

Dream Floors

Above: The rich, warm tones of the wild black cherry floor create an elegant but welcoming ambience, characteristic of antique and river recovered wood floors. Because the wood is grown in the South, almost every third board is curly or figured. This wood is 100% heartwood and is sustainably harvested.

Left: Premium plank ash has beveled edges and ends, and comes with a 25 year residential finish warranty. An engineered product, it can be installed below, on or above ground.

Above: Maple is 12% harder than oak and can bring timeless warmth to any home, with its light, even color and clear, uniform wood grain.

Right: This plank flooring is beautifully hand-crafted and sculpted into the rugged textures of a simple hewn floor. Solid contrast pegs are a terrific detail.

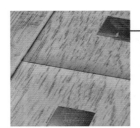

Carpet & Rugs

NOTHING FEELS BETTER UNDERFOOT THAN LUXURIOUS CARPET, an unending array of little fibers nestled together to capture warmth and offer cush, bolstered by a good padding to prolong its life and provide added insulation from noise. Carpeting is a true luxury and with new technology, it is difficult to find one of poor quality. Your goal is to choose the proper carpet or rug for the space you are filling, because the wrong carpet in the wrong location will (obviously) equal something that doesn't perform the way you'd hoped.

As expected, some brands are more hard-wearing than others due to the combination of pile fiber, weights of fiber and density of the pile. Choose a heavy weight, soil hiding fiber, for example, combined with a high density pile over a lighter and looser pile for a longer-lasting covering.

Left: This 100% wool rug is available in both a rectangle and a runner in a variety of sizes.

History in the Making

There is evidence that rugs have been a part of our world's history since years B.C. In fact, an Egyptian fresco of handloom, dated 1480 B.C. was discovered, somewhat recently, in 1953.

By 1000 A.D., Marco Polo confirmed the existence of rugs and rug making techniques, and the craft spread throughout Persia, India, Kabul and other countries.

Sixteenth century Europe saw carpet and rug making begin its fast sprint toward floor covering dominance. In 1791, carpets began inching into the hearts of the American public when William Sprague opened the first carpet mill in Philadelphia, PA. Erasthus Bigelow followed in 1839 when he eternally restructured the industry by inventing the power loom. In just a short decade, he managed to triple production output.

About a hundred years later, synthetic fiber was introduced. Nylon appeared in 1947 and it was as if the sky opened wide. Man made fibers created a wealth of opportunity. Until that time, cotton was the only fiber used in tufted products, and it didn't perform well. Wool was used for woven products—which comprised about ninety percent of carpet output. This introduction of new fibers, along with plentiful improvements in production, caused a flip-flop of popularity. Now, nearly ninety percent of carpets and rugs sold today are tufted.

Left: This contemporary and abstract design was derived from the archives of Warhol's well-known "Pop Art" period. Also available in red.

AndyWarhol®©The Andy Warhol Foundation

58

Today's Carpet & Rugs

Today, the tremendous variety of carpet and rug options can be staggering: pile choices, fiber types and carpet construction options offer endless combinations. And then there's color and pattern: whatever you desire, it's probably available. The whole process can be daunting, so it is important to know your space and not be swayed by a product that will not perform to your expectations. Whatever decision you make, be certain to buy the best you can afford—especially when covering high traffic areas. And then enjoy. Throw yourself down on your new floor and enjoy a good stretch on the plushy goodness that only fiber can bring.

This hard-wearing berber carpeting boasts a larger yarn, especially popular on the West Coast.

The Facts: Carpet

Advantages: Can camouflage and be installed over a well-worn floor, such as wood or vinyl; soft and forgiving, it is the epitome of resiliency; maximum insulation; can be a room's focal point; typically more economical than smooth flooring; sound absorbent; shock absorbing; anti-skid

Disadvantages: Can be affected by moisture; prone to fostering and harboring mold and mildew in dire situations; color can fade if exposed to direct sunlight; pile reversal can cause variations in color; improper dying can cause color transfer; inferior carpet backing can separate from the fiber

Cost: Inexpensive carpeting can be had for as little as two dollars per square foot. Be sure to determine whether the cost includes installation and removal of old flooring materials and also remember that you get what you pay for. Quality, design, fiber type will all factor into the price

Lifespan: Years

Most Appropriate Locations: Bedrooms, living rooms, dens, hallways, staircases

Care & Cleaning: Weekly vacuuming for moderate traffic areas, some manufacturers suggest daily vacuuming for heavily trafficked areas; yearly shampooing, either professional or DIY; remove spots immediately

Left: Considered the new "shag," this broadloom is a high-twist soft frieze.

Above: This frieze construction carpeting was created with 100% BCF nylon. This style is available in 40 colors.

Available in 12 different earthy colors, this product is 100% nylon and available 15' wide.

Berber carpeting is a perfect solution for high traffic areas, as it will hide footprints well and it's easy to vacuum, too.

Good to Know: Fibers & Maintenance

There are two types of carpet fiber in today's market: natural and man-made. Natural includes: wool, silk, jute, coir, sisal and flax. Man-made includes: nylon, polyester, polypropylene (olefin), acrylic and viscose. Use care when selecting your fiber—it will determine how well your carpet will perform over the years when assaulted by foot traffic, pets, spills and other environmental calamities. Also note that some manufacturers offer fiber blends to provide top performance at a terrific price point.

In general, man-made fibers excel at maintaining color, resisting soil and stains and being wear resistant, although wool, the oldest and most well-accepted of the natural fibers, mingles hard wear with exceptional looks.

If you have care for the environment and its precious natural resources, consider carpeting constructed from discarded plastic drink bottles. Instead of plugging up landfills, plastic waste finds new life in beautiful floorcovering, soft and sturdy underfoot.

Premium quality 100% wool, coupled with yarns dyed by the most advanced methods of modern technology, results in subtle color changes and exceptional beauty.

It is important, in order to keep your carpets and rugs at peak beauty, to have a consistent maintenance plan. One point to consider is that carpet is not cleaned just for appearance sake but also for healthy environments. The wonderful thing about fiber is that it is able to trap and filter contaminants from the area in which you normally breathe until they can be removed. If there is a maintenance plan in action for the extraction of dirt and other pollutants in place, you may find that your household is not only beautiful—but healthier as well.

As for appearance, if there is dirt build-up, fibers become abraded and will begin to crush and mat. Your carpet will begin to look ugly, even if there is no pile loss. Take it upon yourself to protect your investment and vacuum regularly, blot and remove spills promptly and have it professionally cleaned periodically.

Dream Floors

Left: The appeal of this modern roomset cannot be denied. Soothing earth tones draw the eye around this restful area.

Above: This two-tone trellis floorcovering carries the Wools of New Zealand brand and has a location guidance rating of extra heavy residential and heavy contract.

Good to Know: Textures
Loop, plush, frieze—what texture is best for you?

Cut & Loop Pile: The definition is particularly self-explanatory. This combination of the best of both worlds offers the possibility for plenty of surface textures including sculptured effects, swirls, squares and more.

Cut Pile Loop: Yarn loops are cut, creating texture and a welcoming feel underfoot. Also most well-known as the shag, it was and still is one of the most popular carpet types. Hides a multitude of sins.

Frieze: Pronounced "free-zay" this tightly curled cut pile masks vacuum cleaner marks and footprints.

Level Loop Pile: Stitched in level, uncut loops of the same height and size, this informal style is very suitable for high-traffic areas. The popular flecked berber style is one example.

Multi-level Loop Pile: Two or three various uncut loop heights create patterns, hide stains and offer a casual look.

Plush: Velvety in appearance due to fibers cut to the same length, this carpet is demanding in its appearance, showing vacuum cleaner marks at will. Luxurious to the touch and beautiful, there is none better, should you wish for a smooth surface.

Saxony: A cut pile, saxony offers a smooth nap. The extra twist in the yarn creates a dense, sophisticated blanket of fiber.

The Facts: Rugs

Advantages: The multitude of standard sizes allow them to fit into almost any area, custom sizes fill any other; pick up and go—the installation of a rug is a matter of unfurling it and stretching it across the floor, providing instantaneous gratification; can be removed and cleaned; can move with you—they're perfect for apartment dwellers; can hide a multitude of flooring sins, adding welcomed warmth, style and protection to areas of high traffic.

Disadvantages: The lack of an anchoring slip-resistant mat underneath will cause any rug to buckle and slide; unsecured edges may be a tripping hazard

Cost: The smallest rugs can cost under five dollars, from there, the sky's the limit

Lifespan: Years

Most Appropriate Locations: Anywhere where something soft underfoot is needed. In entryways, rugs can capture sand and dust that will scrape hardwood floors. In a bathroom, they are a delicate touch underfoot when stepping out of the tub. A grand kilim will be a focal point in a study; a graceful floral in the bedroom can soften the hard lines of an armoire.

Care & Cleaning: Depending upon the size and fabric, various rugs require different types of cleaning methods. Typically, treat as you would carpet: vacuuming, yearly cleaning and immediate clean up of spills.

Left: Rich reds and terracotta tones are the main ingredients iin this beautiful roomset. Accented with bold black and soft shades of green and blue, The use of single-point soft yarn, blended with textured yarn, produces a soft, yet heavy, surface.

Upper right: Eight sheepskins have been expertly matched to form one spectacularly large rug. And although predominently used on the floor as a rug, these soft and luxurious sheepskin pieces may also be used as throws, bedspreads or wherever extra coziness is needed.

Lower right: This rug, reminiscent of a stack of books is hand-knotted of 100% wool and can be custom colored and sized.

Rugs Galore

A short tutorial . . .

Aubusson: The name hails from Aubusson, France, a mid-17th century production center. The first designs were based on Turkish models, but later 19th century rugs took on an English slant. Tapestry; typically portraying flowers, bouquets and architectural themes.

Braided: Thick strips of yarn or fabric are braided into dense ropes, then stitched side-to-side in a variety of circular patterns, creating a reversible rug.

Brocade: An embossed or engraved effect is worked into the rug using heavy twisted yarn tufts on a ground of straight fibers.

Dhurrie: Usually constructed of cotton or wool, this flatwoven rug hails from India.

Drugget: Usually constructed of goat hair, cotton and/or jute, this non-pile rug hails from India and the Balkans.

Fur: Natural fur rugs, such as combed sheepskin, are lush and luxurious. Alpaca, for example, is sheared from an animal; hide rugs (such as cowhide) are culled from those animals discarded by the food industry or from natural circumstances.

Gabbeh: Originally attributed to the nomads of Iran's central Zagros Mountains, who used them in tents. Course rugs adorned with abstract patterns and native images. Recently recognized for their artistic value.

Hand-hooked (Hand-tufted): A rug making process in which yarn is inserted into a pattern-stenciled backing material with a hand-held tufting tool. After the hooking is complete, a second backing is attached to anchor and protect the stitches.

Hand-knotted: Pile yarns are knotted around warp

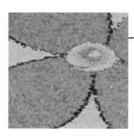

Machine made in Belgium, this cheerful rug perks up a kitchen area stylishly.

fibers that run the length of the rug. The more knots each square inch holds, the more valuable the rug.

Kilim: A flatwoven rug with pileless, smooth surfaced weaving. May be reversible.

Mahal: A rug of medium weave and knot count with a cotton foundation. The name most likely refers to the region of Mahallat. Although of average quality, the design and soft color combination, along with its smooth hand and lustrous wool, elevates its price.

Needlepoint: Wool yarn is worked onto a pattern-stenciled canvas in the same way that, for example, a needlepoint pillow is made. Hand-sewn.

Oriental: Native to the Middle or Far East, these hand-knotted or hand-woven rugs are offered in many patterns and are known for their colorations. Many machine-made rugs, using these same designs, are also referred to as Oriental.

Painted: The application of paint to a rug or canvas. Sealer is placed over the top to protect this fragile medium (*see Alternative section for an example*).

Persian: Rugs named for the primary carpet weaving areas of Iran (Persia). Typically, they are a rich, beautiful wool or silk with curvilinear floral designs. Graceful and intricate, their delicate tones are beautiful and perfectly coordinated.

Rag: Sturdy and colorful, this rug is hand-woven from cotton scraps and is frequently used in the kitchen entryway.

Savonnerie: A hand-knotted rug, French made, pastel in hue, with a floral medallion set on an open field with stuttered borders.

Tibetan Rugs: Rug production in Tibet began as early as the 1700, drawing influence from China and Eastern Turkestan. Using color and pattern to signify function, gold and orange signify religious ceremonial purpose, tiger motifs and patterns were a sign of power and authority and maroon covered the floors of monasteries, for example. All wool; and hand-knotted using a Tibetan technique resembling a continuous system of knots.

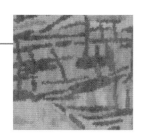

Left: Designed by Stephanie Odegard in cooperation with the Metropolitan Museum of Art, this hand spun wool griffin rug was hand-knotted in Nepal and measures 5' 11" x 8' 8".

Above: This classic-style Oriental rug is cross-woven in Belgium of 100% New Zealand wool carries a five star wear rating, qualifying it for commercial use.

Left: A 100% semi-worsted New Zealand wool, this parchment colored rug was hand-tufted in India.

Middle: Rugmark is an internationally recognized nonprofit organization working to end illegal child labor in the carpet industry and offer educational opportunities to children in Nepal, India and Pakistan. To that end, 1⅜% of the purchase of this carpet goes to the Rugmark Foundation.

Right: One hundred percent polypropylene and power loom woven, this rug is not only beautiful, but hard wearing.

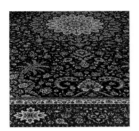 

Above left: One hundred percent polypropylene and machine made in Egypt, this beautiful rug is available in a variety of sizes, including a stair runner.

Below left: With a 60 millimeter pile height, this ivory six-sheepskin rug goes through a 42 step tanning process—a process that also shows a great deal of consideration for its impact on the environment.

Below right: This rug offers both warranties in residential usage as well as stain resistance but better yet, provides warmth and a lovely cushion underfoot, softening the room without drawing attention away from all of the lovely wood.

This page: Made in the United States, this area rug is power loom woven and constructed of sturdy nylon fiber. Available in both rectangles and runners.

Above: Throughout his life, Andy Warhol was consistently fascinated by the magic and beauty of nature—insects, animals, sunsets and flowers. This rug was inspired by a series of flower drawings that Warhol created in the 1950s when he worked as a commercial artist. AndyWarhol®©The Andy Warhol Foundation

Left: This Dupont Stainmaster Xlife BCF nylon carpet offers a soothing backdrop to the interior furnishings.

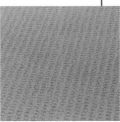

Above: A relaxed, natural color scheme is enhanced with a subtly twilight-toned, patterned carpet.

Right: This elegant carpeting is one hundred percent Anso Caress nylon imbued with 3m Scotchguard Stain Release.

Comfort rugs for the uncluttered domain. Casual textures and tonal colors give your room a beckoning, blended atmosphere. One hundred percent New Zealand wool, this rug is available in 114 custom colors.

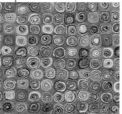

Small jewel-like swirls of color sweep this rug with zest and playfulness. Lamontage, patented medium for creating textiles, combines the ancient art of felting with modern technology and materials. The name of this innovative method is derived from "lamina" for layering and "montage" for image. Photo courtesy of Simon Feldman.

This rug feels like chenille and has the look of an antique Oriental rug. Textured and uneven, its stylized motifs feature complex dyes and designs from eras long past.

With a fine pencil point finish (850,000 points per square meter) to provide superior definition and detail, this Exellan fiber area rug is available in rectangles and runners, and offers moisture-proof pile for easy maintenance.

Dream Floors

Left: This cut pile berber construction created with 100% BCF nylon is available in nine colors.

Above: Create interest in any room by adding patterned carpeting. Suddenly, the focal point is the beautiful floor.

Left: This gorgeous rug boasts a wonderful coloration and cross woven construction with up to 36 colors in 100% heat set polypropylene. The reds, greens, browns and plums that vary from soft to deep tones—a compelling combination.

Center: Hand-knotted and dyed with only natural and vegetal Swiss dyes, this supple rug is made with a blend of silk and wool, offering unrivalled depth and nuance of color.

Right: The patented Lamontage product is specially created by blending and mixing custom dyed fibers, resulting in a rich palette of over 600 hues, which are then manipulated to generate intricate color possibilities. The rug artisans blend, layer, cut and hand create each design using special hand-held needles. Photo courtesy of Simon Feldman.

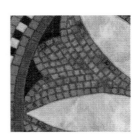

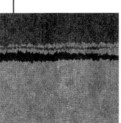
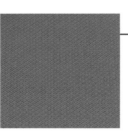

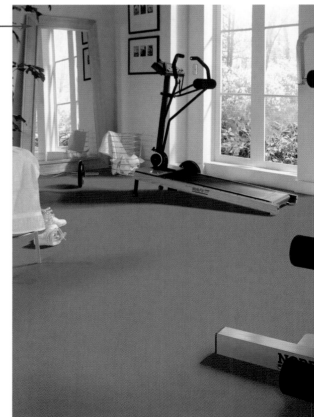

Above: This lovely rug is characterized by bold designs, fewer color planes and a blend of wools. Thick and plush, it is available in uncommon color combinations for those with a strong sense of individuality.

Right: Try carpeting in an exercise room for a more relaxed look. Blue is also a terrific color to sooth your head while you exercise your body.

Left: Broadloom carpet can unify an interior and make multiple spaces work in tandem.

Below: Power-loom woven, this rug was designed with a consumers' lifestyle in mind. Minimal care and a variety of sizes make this handsome piece perfect for everyday use.

 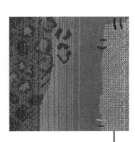

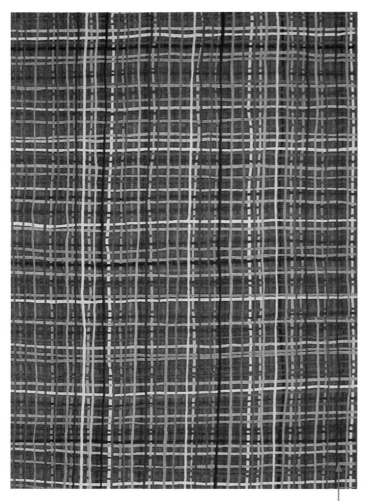

This modern, playful and vibrant rug celebrates colors with an earthy shade of red background and interwoven gold, rusty orange, blues and greens that shimmer with originality.
Photo courtesy of Simon Feldman.

Hailing from Belgium, this rug is made of Exellan, a fiber that combines the best characteristics of wool, nylon and polypropylene. Put through a specific delustre process in order to make the yarn feel and look more like wool, it will not, however, pill like wool rugs. Wear resistant, permanently antistatic and mothproof, it is colorfast and durable—a true value.

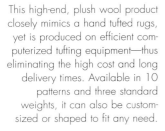

This high-end, plush wool product closely mimics a hand tufted rugs, yet is produced on efficient computerized tufting equipment—thus eliminating the high cost and long delivery times. Available in 10 patterns and three standard weights, it can also be custom-sized or shaped to fit any need.

The colors of this rug were influenced by the verdant colors of northern Europe. With a design derived from the vast royal history of the Highlands region, its special construction was designed to replicate classic Axminster carpets of the region.

Resilient

RESILIENT FLOORING IS JUST THAT: hard-wearing, pliant and enduring. Offering a slight "give" when walked upon, resilients create a yielding and comfortable feel underfoot. A category consisting of vinyl, linoleum, cork and rubber, resilient is most often found in areas where flooring may need to take a beating: the kitchen, laundry room, bathroom, mudroom and even playrooms. Of the four types of resilient products, vinyl wins hands down in popularity due to its ease of installation and lower price point, but linoleum, for instance, is making headway due to resurging interest in retro interiors and its "cradle-to-cradle" natural ingredients, and cork is receiving accolades for its environmentally-friendly sustainable harvesting techniques.

Get the look of oxidized slatestone without the huge expense when you opt for durable, stain-resistant vinyl sheet flooring.

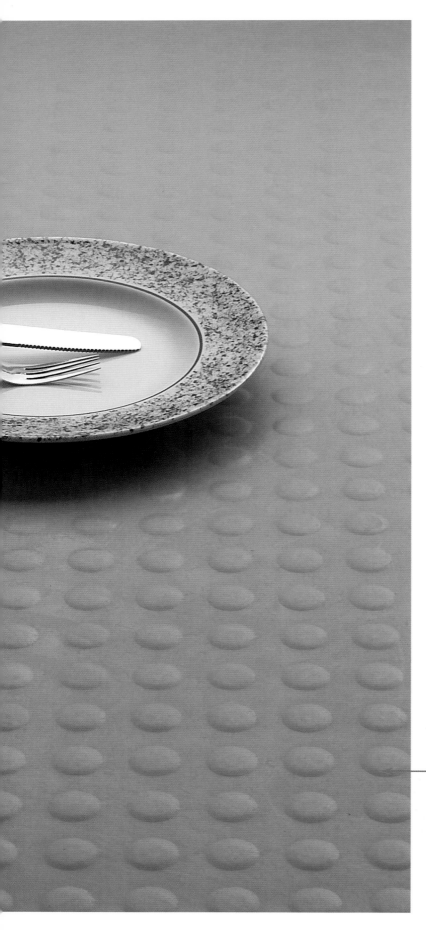

History in the Making

The love affair with resilient flooring began in the early nineteenth century when experimentation with raw materials such as cork and rubber gave way to Kamptulicon (*kampto* from the Greek word for "flexible"), a British invention that combined the two products. By 1862, this combination of India rubber mixed with finely ground cork was causing a sensation. Though not attractive being it had to rely on its natural pigmentation (that of a muddy grayish brown), more changes were underway. At about the same time, Brit Frederick Walton invented Kampticon (to capitalize on the already known Kamptulicon), but then renamed his product Linoleum (Latin for flax—*linum*—and oil—*oleum*).

In the meantime, rubber floor tiles were patented by a Philadelphia architect, Frank Furness, in 1894. While they were easy to clean and install, the tiles stained and deteriorated readily.

In 1904, the first cork tile flooring was introduced to widespread acclaim. It was the most popular category of resilient-style flooring in the 1920s, despite being porous, pricey and limited in colors and patterns. In the 1940s, architect Frank Lloyd Wright specified cork floors for his Fallingwater, in Pennsylvania.

In 1933, vinyl composition tile was exhibited at the Century of Progress Exposition in Chicago, Ill. but wasn't extensively marketed until after the war years. As it gathered steam, it quickly annihilated its competitors, making it, by the 1970s, the most popular hard surface flooring choice.

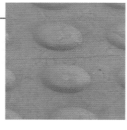

Rubber tile is environmentally friendly, totally PVC free and is manufactured of safe 100 percent vulcanized rubber.

Today's Resilients

Today, while the choices for resilient flooring are still very firmly seeded in these four categories, technological advances have done away with many of the negatives and made these products a worthwhile investment. Second only to carpet in floor covering sales, the number of colors and patterns; the outstanding creativity waiting to be employed in interior decoration using resilient cork, rubber, vinyl or linoleum, is an enhancement to any interior.

Finally, an added bonus is that resilient flooring in general requires little maintenance—mostly just a damp mop and a customary sweep, but that regular and attentive maintenance is the best way to keep it long lasting and lustrous.

Vinyl tile offers a multitude of combinations to make floors the center of attention. This floor is truly eye-catching!

Vinyl

Available in both tile and sheet form, there is no better value than vinyl flooring. Durable, stain resistant, easy to install and comfortable underfoot, vinyl is extremely water-resistant and available in a variety of attractive colors and patterns. A new development in its production could be considered the equivalent of photocopying: creating vinyl tiles that resemble anything—green grass, wet rocks and fabric, for instance.

It is available in two different wear layers: Urethane (a mid- to upper-end finish that protects the printed layer from most scuffs, spills and potential staining) and Poly-vinyl Chloride (PVC, a more basic wear layer that while protective, does not safeguard the printed layer as effectively).

Once shunned for its low durability factor (early vinyl carried only the pattern in its top layer), it has undergone a fabulous makeover, making it tougher than ever.

Above: This vinyl sheet flooring is available in a 12' width and features a patented no-wax wear surface.

Left: Honister slate, a weathered, stone look replicated in vinyl, was inspired by a green slate quarried in the Cumbrian Mountains.

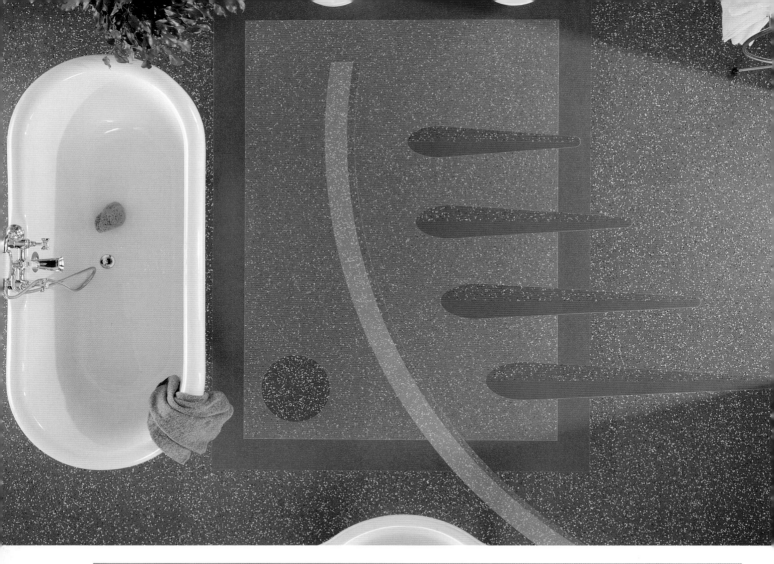

The Facts: Vinyl Sheet & Tile

Advantages: Low cost (adhesive backed tiles can be acquired for as little as .49¢ per square foot); very easy for the DIY handy person to install; highly water resistant; low maintenance; pliable enough to resolve slightly unlevel areas in a floor; easy to replace when damaged

Disadvantages: Traffic areas will yellow over time due to oil transferred from the sole of the shoe to the floor; seldom recycled, it is more commonly disposed of in land fills; low-end varieties may off-gas VOCs (volatile organic compounds); somewhat difficult to repair; low-end varieties can tear easily

Cost: .49 to $10 per square foot depending upon whether it is sheet or tile vinyl

Lifespan: Years

Most Appropriate Locations: Kitchen, bathroom, mud room, laundry areas, playrooms, finished basements

Care & Cleaning: Remove surface dirt with a mop or vacuum; clean with just a damp mop.

Left: This commercial grade safety flooring is designed to help reduce the risk of slipping in high spillage or consistantly wet areas. Incorporating silicon carbide, quartz and aluminum oxide particles, it is also enhanced with antibacterial protection.

Above: Select maple-like vinyl sheet flooring offers stunningly realistic, clear and vibrant floor designs.

Resilient: Vinyl Sheet & Tile

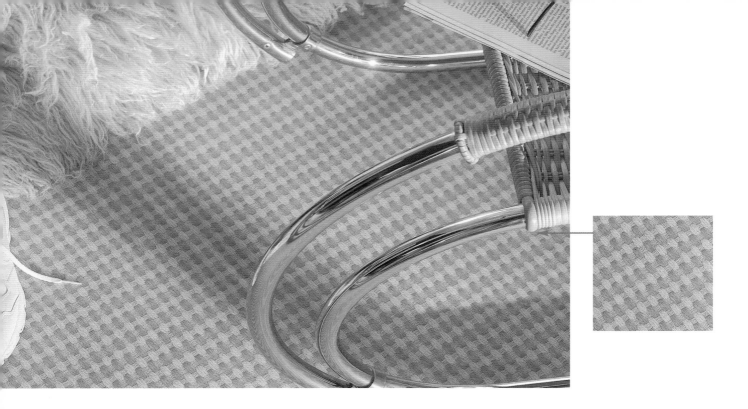

Above: Tropical weave bamboo vinyl sheeting features a patented no-wax wear surface and a 15-year limited warranty.

Below: Available in five different natural colors, the Carolina slate-style vinyl sheet flooring has built-in stain and soil repellent to help keep floors looking their best.

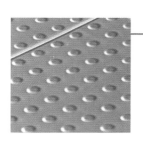

Above: Extra thick construction makes this vinyl sheet flooring exceedingly durable and hard wearing. Available in multi-white, multi-color and multi-pastel to fit any interior's color scheme.

Below: This vinyl tile offers a unique 3-D effect within its smooth finish. Special bevelled stripping is available; tiles must be tessellated. Mod!

Above: This upscale look faithfully mimics the appearance of real stone, ceramic and wood in a 9" x 9" paver that incorporates a diamond inset keystone.

Left: This 3¼" wide oak plank design replicated in vinyl sheeting is available in cherry, saddle, butterscotch, fawn and prairie. Memories™ has an overall thickness of .065 inch, felt backing, a 10-year warranty and ToughGuard® performance, it is guaranteed not to rip, tear or gouge from normal household use for the life of the warranty.

Dream Floors

Dream Floors

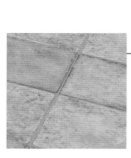

Left: Marquina and Biancone, lovely black and white stone-look tiles can be used alone or combined for a checkerboard effect.

Above: Available in five earth tones, this vinyl sheet flooring has a patented nylon and aluminum oxide reinforced surface for unmatched wear and scratch resistance.

Left: Vinyl sheet flooring is easy to clean and always looks beautiful.

Middle: Stain resistant vinyl sheet flooring mimics the appearance of red oak.

Right: With a super touch finish, cotswold limestone vinyl tile with beveled edge complements the quarry finished concrete look vinyl tile. Available in a variety of sizes.

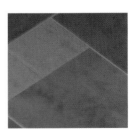

Cork

Harvested from the bark of the cork oak tree in a sustainable manner (the bark is stripped from the tree approximately every nine years), this renewable resource is available in either tile, sheet good or plank tongue-in-groove format. It is also available in four different types of readiness: (1) unfinished, stained and ready to urethane, (2) unfinished, unstained and ready to urethane, (3) pre-finished and urethane covered and (4) pre-finished and vinyl covered.

While it is susceptible to damage from high heels and animal claws, it is less vulnerable than hardwood, as the "give" in its cellular structure allows some bounce back.

Beautiful and environmentally-friendly, cork has only recently entered the public consciousness again in just the past few years. However, with more individuals looking for products that are environmentally sensitive and durable—as well as attractive—it is no doubt that cork will be a product specified with more frequency.

Above: Cork is a fire inhibitor that does not spread flame or produce toxic gases upon combustion and is available in both glue-down tile and floating floor plank.

Right: This checkerboard pattern shows off the varying beauty of four tile colors in this Batimore, MD residence designed by Swanston & Associates. Photo by Eric Oxendorf.

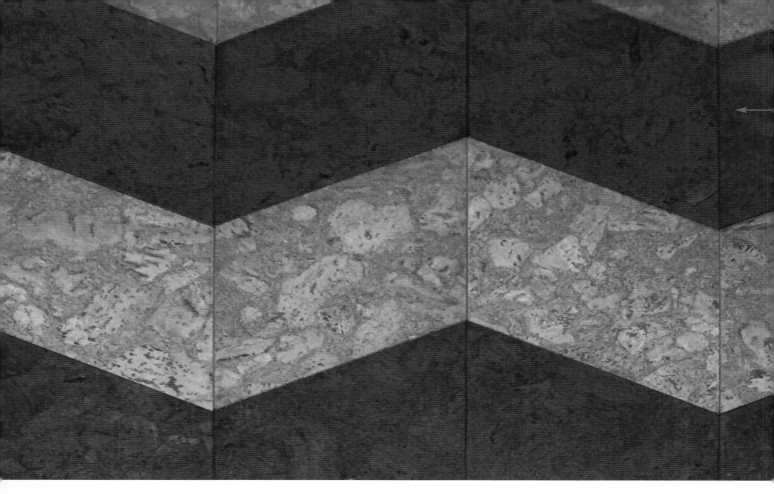

The Facts: Cork

Advantages: Comfortable to stand on; easy installation and maintenance; sound absorbent; durable; antimicrobial; resistant to mold and mildew; fire-resistant; its natural look will complement any interior

Disadvantages: While it is moisture resistant, cork is affected by changes in humidity and temperature and will expand or contract slightly in reaction to climactic changes; color will fade over time (as wood does) so it is best installed away from direct sunlight; not for heavy traffic as it is susceptible to damage from repeated abrasion; may emit an "earthy" odor

Cost: From five to six dollars per square foot (parquet); from six to eight dollars per square foot for floating (plank) floor

Lifespan: Up to eighty years with proper maintenance

Most Appropriate Locations: Kitchen, family rooms, music rooms, home offices; commercial properties such as libraries and churches where the acoustical benefits are well employed

Care & Cleaning: Regular sweeping and damp mopping. Refurbish approximately once a year to eight years (based on the type of finish you have selected) depending upon foot traffic to reinforce the protective layer and restore original luster.

Left: Heavy pressure does not break down or destroy the tiny air cells that are unique to cork; pressure only compresses the air within the cells. The cork begins to spring back when the pressure is removed.

Above: Acoustically sound and aesthetically unique, cork floors are typically available in four finishes (polyurethane, oiled, waxed or unfinished).

Above: This cork floor is protected with five coats of UV cured acrylic finish. This durable floor is easy to care for with regular sweeping and/or vacuuming. Wipe up spills immediately and periodically apply a no buff one-step hardwood floor cleaner to retain the original luster. No wet maintenance required!

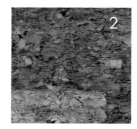

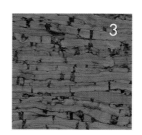

Box 1: Rectangles of whitewashed colored cork with accents of slate gray and amethyst cork are truly eye-catching.

Box 2: Wide mosaic specialty tile is available in two thicknesses and can be custom finished in gloss polyurethane.

Box 3: Available with a matte urethane finish or unfinished, this contemporary tile from is ⅜" thick and available in 12" x 12" sections.

Box 4: The beauty of long-lasting cork. Installed in 1927, this cork flooring in traditional light and dark is as lustrous as the day it was laid.

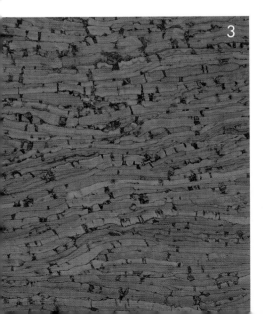

Dream Floors

Left: Cork flooring provides a comfortable and beautiful resilient cushion underfoot. In addition to being resilient, cork is inherently hypoallergenic and anti-microbial, characteristics rendering it ideal for use in kitchens.

Below: Traditional medium toned tiles are installed in this Philadelphia, PA Historical Society library.

Above: Light and medium colored traditional cork tile is offered in two sizes and thicknesses, and three finishes. Custom options are also available.

Box 1: Cork tiles in a herringbone style shine with a cut in trim and outer border.

Box 2: Natural, unfinished cork ³⁄₁₆" thick, was coated with urethane post installation to seal the cork and keep it beautiful and resilient.

Box 3: Wide swaths of red and green cork create vibrancy in this Beechwood, OH restaurant. Photo by Eric Oxendorf.

Box 4: The beauty of cork mosaic thin strip is shown in this Toronto, Ontario advertising agency.

Cork bark is harvested from the cork oak tree.
Photo courtesy of Expanko Inc.

Good to Know: Cork

- The "Nine Year" law, passed in the 1930s, forbade cork bark harvesting at intervals of no less than nine years, so maximum regrowth can occur and trees are not compromised.
- Cork may not be harvested until the tree has reached a diameter of sixty centimeters.
- One with nature: Using hand tools to harvest the bark is still the preferred method.
- The honeycomb cellular structure of hexagonal cells makes cork naturally resilient—over ninety percent of the material inside each cell is airy gas. It's that

Left: Two very unique patterns combine to create a dynamic swirl of impact in a Madison, WI beauty salon. Photo by Eric Oxendorf

The specialized cellular structure of cork makes it naturally resilient and lightweight. *Shown*: Raw cork and tiles.
Photo courtesy of Dodge Cork.

wonderfully soft feeling underfoot—certainly not spongy, however—that makes cork a natural in areas where someone might be standing for long periods of time. Consider, too, that the encapsulated cells are a terrific insulator, capturing heat to maximize heat savings.

Right: Natural cork with mocha stripes is displayed at Vanderbilt University's Owen Graduate School of Management in Nashville. Photo by Eric Oxendorf

Rubber

While rubber flooring has been around for ages, a new type of rubber flooring made from recycled automotive tires, post industrial waste, rubber and virgin rubber has been gaining the popular vote. It has been said that one tire is the equivalent of five square feet of rubber tile. So, not only does recycled rubber flooring solve a tremendous environmental problem—what to do with all of the old tires that before, were disposed of by incineration—but it also offers consumers exceptional flooring benefits. And not to worry about that dirty black "tire" color. Colored synthetic rubber is mixed in to create the most vibrant of tones. If you are looking for flooring with long-term value and feel that rubber should be underfoot—not underground—look no further than rubber.

Above: This rubber tile is available in an oversized 24" x 24", allowing fewer seams and less waste.

Right: From lobbies to lounges, to malls to museums, rubber flooring works anywhere. Made from high-quality, medium and jumbo-sized reprocessed EPDM rubber granules, it is sophisticated and long-lasting.

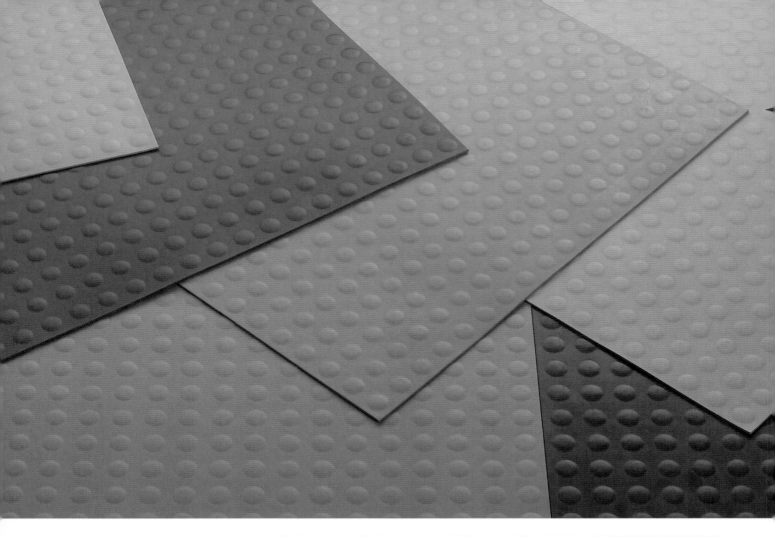

The Facts: Rubber

Advantages: Clear, uniform colors; excellent resilience; quiet and sound absorbent; durable; does not contain any PVCs or halogens; has an extremely dense, smooth surface as compared to the other resilient categories; effectively dirt repellant; recyclable

Disadvantages: Expensive, but cost is recouped through years of use; may be slippery when wet; must be installed above the grade; could be damaged by grease or tough detergents

Cost: Approximately $2 to $12 dollars per square foot

Lifespan: Decades

Most Appropriate Locations: Very suitable for extra heavy traffic, including forklifts and unending foot traffic. This could include commercial locations such as warehouses, gymnasiums and airports but could also transfer to residential applications such as exercise rooms, bathrooms and laundry rooms

Care & Cleaning: Rubber can be damaged by strong detergents, so use only water and a mop for best cleaning.

Left: Quiet underfoot, this rubber tile is available in over 100 colors. With matching stair treads and wall base systems, it is compression moulded at 2000 pounds per square inch.

Above: The corporate headquarters of the Princess Cruise Lines in Valencia, CA show off a cork/rubber blend of resilient flooring. All raw and finished material waste produced during production is recycled back into the product. In addition, used XCR3 is also recyclable.

Lower left: Rubber flooring, shown here at the AllSteel Corporate Headquarters in Chicago, IL, is made from a unique blend of recycled tires, post industrial waste rubber and virgin rubber.

Lower right: A collage of colors. Designed for high traffic areas where durability and easy maintenance are desired, rubber flooring offers a unique palette of neutrals, primary and predominately black colors.

Linoleum

Although gloriously colorful and wildly creative at initial installation, linoleum was largely delegated to being a trend of the moment (read: 1950s) due to its propensity to fade over time, as well as issues of wearability. By the 1970s, when the invention of no-wax vinyl flooring become *de rigueur* for every American household, linoleum was history. All production in the U.S. ceased by 1974.

Yet, today's linoleum, also one of the oldest "earth-friendly" flooring materials around (being derived from a combination of renewable products such as linseed oil, cork and wood flour, pigments and pine resins), has turned over a new and very colorful leaf. Improved technologies, brought about since production began again in the mid-1980s, have allowed for better color consistency and brighter colors, and also, the movement toward environmentally-friendly products (which vinyl is not) played a large part in its resurgence.

While the connotation of "tacky" may still stick (undeservedly) to this particular brand of flooring, it is only because old habits die hard. It was the splendid experimentation in colors and patterns, bizarre boomerang patterns festooned with starbursts and frankly faux woodgrain patterns resembling crayon on grocery bags that intimidated the more genteel crowd. But that was then. Think earth-friendly; think linoleum.

Above: Peach, beige and green linoleum offers the fine marbling look of classic linoleum in a retro pattern.

Right: Deep, rich marbling reminiscent of stone makes linoleum sheet flooring a work of art.

The Facts: Linoleum

Advantages: Softer and warmer than vinyl; naturally-occurring anti-static properties which repel dust; deep color saturation, so a gouge in the flooring will not be as apparent as with vinyl; recyclable; constructed of all-natural ingredients

Disadvantages: Can discolor or deform when introduced to extreme heat. Tile seams may collect dirt and/or debris, which could encourage bacterial growth. Seams can also loosen when improperly installed and wear down over time. Professional installation recommended

Cost: $3–$22 dollars per square foot, installed. Also depends upon whether it is sheet or tile

Lifespan: Thirty to 40 years

Most Appropriate Locations: Kitchen, mudroom, laundry areas, playrooms

Care & Cleaning: Remove surface dirt with a mop or vacuum; clean with just a damp mop. Apply an acrylic or wax sealer once a year to keep luster high.

Left: A hopscotch of colorful linoleum tiles energize this office setting.

Upper right: Lilac-hued stripes pop in this line of durable linoleum.

Lower right: Beautiful, clean and allergen-free, linoleum is one of the oldest "earth-friendly" flooring materials available.

Flax, above, is the flower which produces linseed oil, a component (about 30 percent) of linoleum. In fact, the word *linem* is the Latin term for flax. Photo courtesy of Forbo Linoleum Inc.

Good to Know: Linoleum

- Completely biodegradable, linoleum is gentle on the environment, as it is made entirely of natural products.
- Because linoleum promotes healthy living, it is also a good choice for those who suffer from allergies, asthma or other environmental irritants. Hypoallergenic, linoleum does not emit gasses, is naturally antistatic (thus repelling dust, dirt and pollens) and has antibacterial properties.
- When linoleum is installed, be aware of ambering, a temporary visual yellowing that will disappear (and not reappear) when exposed to sunlight. To test, cover half of one piece with cardboard and put in direct sunlight for one hour. Remove the covering and you will immediately see the change.

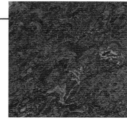

- Don't let them fool you— linoleum is *not* vinyl. Many people still confuse the two products.

Ultrasound and water jet cutting techniques enable artists to create exciting patterns and motifs, such as this cuppa joe at a student union coffee shop.

Far left edge: Eye-popping blue linoleum delivers random marbling for a completely unique decorating experience.

Right: A vibrant combination of five different colors in this educational environment keeps students moving and awake on even the most brain taxing of days.

Left: You might think it's a rug coupled with wood inlay—but it's linoleum!

Middle: Deep mottled red linoleum flooring offers dramatic impact.

Right: This silver linoleum creates a high tech backdrop for a sleek office environment.

Dream Floors

Laminate

YOU CAN THANK THE INGENIOUS SCANDINAVIANS FOR THE HOTTEST FLOOR TREATMENT developed in the past twenty-five years: laminate. Easy to install, resistant to dents, stains, cigarette burns and also known as "the great pretender" due to its ability to replicate many other kinds of more expensive flooring, laminate is perfect for high traffic pet-and-child households.

Sales of laminate flooring hit the billion dollar-plus mark for the first time in 2003, showing a 32.5 percent growth rate in 2003 alone. Eighty percent of these sales went toward replacing an existing floor. And the raves about this easy, versatile product continue. A "floating" floor, it is installed on top of any existing floor—not glued, but locked together to form seamless perfection.

Upper, middle and lower left: Laminate is ultimately resistant to dents, stains and cigarette burns—and can even be installed over an existing floor.

Adjacent: This rendition of a classic red oak floor put together with an EasyConnect system, in which the planks lock mechanically together using the simple method of angling and lowering planks into place, versus tapping.

History in the Making

In Sweden in the early 1980s, laminate flooring came into focus when, first used as counter top or wall paneling applications, it made the logical next step . . . down. At first, much needed to be overcome to make a laminate flooring material that would outperform anything on a table or countertop. In the next few years, however, technical research discovered ways to make this flooring over twenty times stronger than its original embodiment. Thus, the first laminate flooring materials emerged. Additionally, packaging was a huge plus—instead of the long planks of traditional solid wood, four-foot strips of laminate, boxed and lightweight, were easy to transport.

Laminate crossed over from Europe in the early 1990s and took North America by storm, surpassing European sales by leaps and bounds. Brand names like Pergo® became part of the American lexicon—indeed, almost synonymous for laminate.

This elegant flooring shows off a recent innovation in laminate technology: embossed-in-register texture.

Today's Laminates

Laminates consist of four layers: the wear layer, which, in essence, is the protective finish that covers the "photograph"—also known as the decorative (beauty) layer. The third layer is the fiberboard core, which provides resistance to impact and also stability and finally, a back layer, which helps with moisture resistance and also offers some stability as well. Recently, two impressive modifications have been made: the first, a movement from the use of a more expensive high-pressure laminate to the cost-efficient direct laminate. ("Direct" meaning that the layers are bonded concurrently under pressure and heat versus in steps involving pressure, heat and glue.) Second, a change to a "click" joint assembly, rather than glue joints, for ease of installation. Underlayment has also improved upon the "hollow" sound once made by installed laminates, improving acoustical properties as well.

As for the beauty of the product—it has made great strides in offering a variety of looks. From wood to stone to anything else desired, the number of pattern options for laminate is limited only by its producers.

Below: Burled oak-style laminate creates a warm, inviting area for the heart of the home.

The Facts: Laminate

Advantages: Can replicate many other kinds of flooring such as wood, stone or tile; extremely durable and resistant to stain; easy to install on any grade level; great for the do-it-yourselfer due to glueless locking system option; resists expansion and contraction due to changes in humidity; can be installed over an existing floor

Disadvantages: While it can imitate the look of another product, it doesn't necessarily sound or feel like it; cannot be refinished, sanded or stripped; not soft underfoot; knock off products will show seams

Cost: $2–$20 per square foot

Lifespan: 10 to 25 years, even considered a lifetime guarantee depending upon the grade

Most Appropriate Locations: Kitchen, baths, living rooms, entryways, high traffic areas are fine

Care & Cleaning: Sweep to eliminate dust and dirt, use a manufacturer's recommended cleaner for occasional spot cleaning to keep luster high or a solution of one part vinegar to two parts water. No stripping of wax build-up necessary.

Left: Wood-like textures follow the grain of the laminate plank for a look that resembles real wood.

Upper right: This laminate flooring shows significant color design variation from plank to plank, creating an antique look.

Lower right: Honey red oak is a laminate with a sturdy reputation and a strong personality. Available in three lengths separated by a subtle v-groove, it features a rich and stately sheen that will never need waxing or polishing.

Laminate

Good to Know: Laminates

- Laminate planks typically need a "curing" time of about 48 hours in the space they are to be installed, so the product can adjust to the relative humidity of the room
- For a beautiful look, have the planks installed in the same direction as the outdoor light enters the room
- Laminates are considered the most impervious of the floorings to outside influences such as foot traffic, spills, cigarette burns, UV rays, bacteria and wheels from chairs and suitcases.
- Ask for underlayment that helps to replicate the lower decibel sound put forth by hardwood. Installed under the laminate planks, this underlayment also helps level a floor, ensuring proper installation.
- Consider laminate tile . . . yes, *tile*. With the look of genuine tile, there are other benefits, such as a softer feel underfoot and an absence of the messy, lengthy installation process.
- Ask for products that use EIR (embossed-in-register) texturing for a more realistic look. Add to that the new beveled edge look which mimics the edge of a solid wood product and you will be truly amazed at how realistic this product appears.
- Wood/laminate hybrids are making way in the market, in which a wood veneer is used in place of the typical decor (photo) layer.

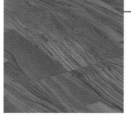

The latest in laminates offering three-strip designs, it is categorized by its rich colors, high definition and great performance. Backed with a 30 year residential warranty, this floor is tough and beautiful.

Above: Closely following the design and the relief of natural wood graining, this natural varnished maple laminate shows beauty at its peak.

Below: Exceptional looks coupled with a 20 year limited warranty are the hallmarks of this sturdy floor covering.

Above: Medium cherry laminate, incorporating Lustergard Plus surface protection, provides exceptional resistance to scuffs and scratches—keeping the floor looking newer, longer.

Laminate

Brazil nut laminate shows the embossed-in-register surface texturing, in which the texture is embossed in register with the underlying decor, creating a very realistic product.

Upper left: With a plank size of approximately 7½" x 47" and with 45 colors of various wood species, this golden-tone laminate offers endless combinations.

Middle left: Dark varnished cherry laminate is sophisticated and luxurious, yet strong enough for the heaviest of traffic.

Lower Left: The excellent durability of this flooring, coupled with the warm, subtle look of wood, creates one of the best choices in floor coverings today.

Below: Brazilian cherry laminate planks lock together perfectly to ensure close-fitting seams and can also be taken up and reinstalled five times.

The look of tile in a laminate. No messy grout to contend with during installation!

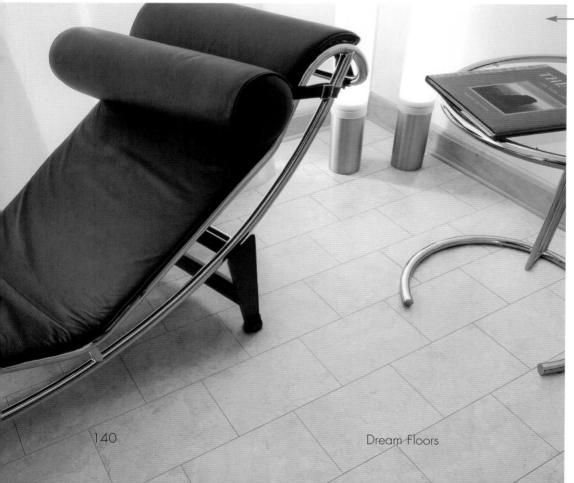

If your foot traffic is continuous, consider commercial grade laminate, such as this travertine-style laminate.

This laminate features the Armalock Installation System, meaning no gluing is necessary and better yet—touts a 25 year limited warranty.

The subtle combination of three plank lengths ensures a realistic and varied effect and a beautiful finished product that will last for years.

Above left: Laminate stair treads can be an important feature in the home because stairs often undergo more stress than the floor itself. These stair treads are an aesthetic, practical and cost-effective solution to the problem of heavy traffic. Easy to install and able to cover most existing surfaces, they are also suitable for unfinished steps and are available in the 45 colors.

Middle Left: This laminate flooring is a replica of the real merbau, a wood species native to the South Pacific. Although principally used for flooring, its warm and refined appearance make it a valuable species for many interior applications.

Lower Left: Featuring a unique locking mechanism that makes it possible to create a variety of design patterns, this floor covering is uniquely beautiful.

Below: Microbevel laminate has small bevels at the edges of each plank, simulating a natural wood look. The slight v-groove that the beveling creates between planks gives the floor an authentic appearance.

Dream Floors

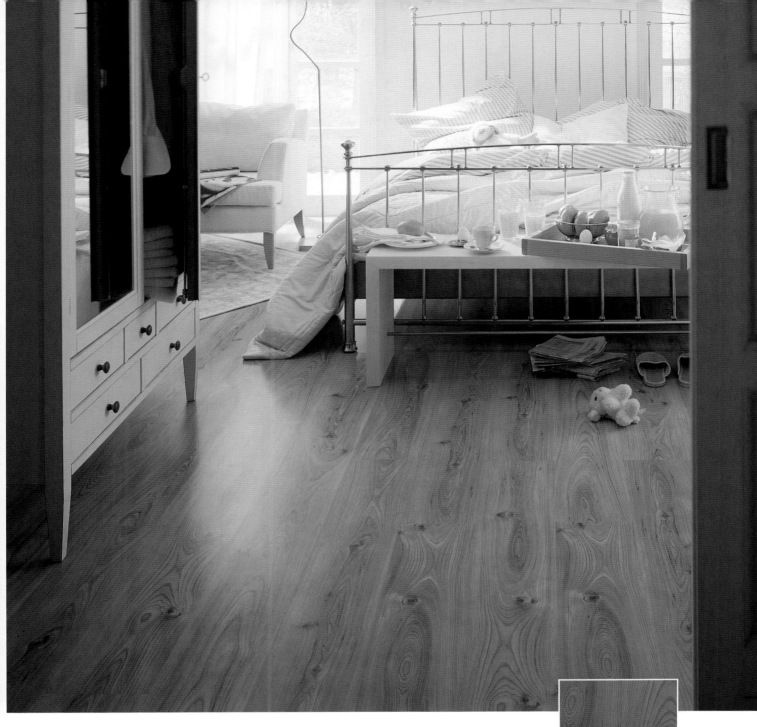

Above: Elm laminate flooring is a full plank design, eight millimeters thick, in a generous 50.63" long by 7.64" wide. Note the realistic knot holes—so beautiful!

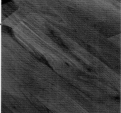

Above: Stunning color changes and a warm, winning surface is a stylish for any home, be it traditional or ultra modern—or somewhere in between.

The natural beauty of stone-look laminate tile.

Registered embossing captures the texture of real tile. Joint Guard replicates authentic-looking grout lines. Durable construction features a patented integral mechanical locking system.

Top: Cream colored tile in the bathroom offers a soothing retreat.

Bottom: Earth-toned laminate tile is perfect for a sunny getaway, bringing the colors of the outdoors in.

Above: Realistic surface textures coupled with Isowaxx, a moisture resistent substance that is injected into the joints of every plank, improves the moisture performance of laminate floors and allows warranty in moisture-prone areas such as entryways and kitchens.

Right: Butterscotch-toned oak laminate offers a smooth, warm and lovely contrast to the darker-toned bedroom furnishings.

Laminate

Dream Floors

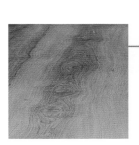

Upper left: This laminate flooring offers a Lifetime Five Star Plus Limited Warranty which stands behind the durability of your flooring for as long as you own it.

Lower left: The staggered color patterns of Vermont maple cinnamon laminate offers beauty, as well as easy installation—a stellar combination.

Upper right: The embossed texture on this floor covering provides the look and feel of hardwood as well as offers Sound Inhibitor™ to imitate hardwood's natural sound.

Lower right: Deep grain walnut laminate is a rendition of black walnut, a wood species most commonly found in the interior of eastern North America. Its strength, hardness, silky sheen, deep tone and coarse grain make a character-rich floor, replicating the feel of surfaces typically found on authentic hardwood floors.

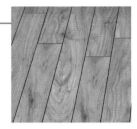

Left: Strip golden pecan laminate complements a soothing checkboard tile backsplash and harmonizes perfectly with the multi-toned wall squares.

Below: A laminate stair system couples with flooring to create an attractive, innovative solution for coordinating stairs and flooring.

Above: Glueless flooring systems offer the beauty of wood with the ease of maintenance only laminate can bring.

Left: Enhancements such as Sound-Inhibitor, a pre-attached underlayment and moisture-resistant features make this birch replicate a wonderful choice for a study area.

Above: Emerald slate laminate is reminiscent of traditional green slate tones and hues in 16" x 16" tiles. Coordinated "grout" serves to replicate typical installations found throughout North America.

Right: Notice how the textures in this oak-style laminate follow the natural grain of real wood. This looks entirely authentic but costs less than real wood.

Wide laminate planks in a
deep cognac tone bring rich
elegance to any room.

This extra durable floor exhibits
one of the thickest laminates
available, including a Water-
Safety Edge Seal, which inhibits
moisture from penetrating seams.

Oak laminate offers thicker premium core material, providing
great stability and better
impact and moisture resistance.

Glueless laminate flooring boasts
high scratch resistance and
durable surface features to allow
full enjoyment of your life at
home, no matter how rough and
tumble.

Left: Glue-free technology and 25 Year Triple-Plus warranty against wear-through, stains, fading and water damage from promptly removed everyday spills makes this laminate collection a great value.

Above: Snap together glueless laminate exhibits rich, warm wood-grains in a wide selection of colors, including beech (*shown*). A lifetime limited warranty assures long-lasting beauty.

Tile & Stone

EARTH. WATER. FIRE. AIR. THE ESSENTIAL ELEMENTS OF LIFE. These are also the elements of tile, a flooring material that has spanned centuries, celebrating color and pattern unmatched by any other flooring category. Glazed or unglazed, extruded or pressed dust, slab, field, tumbled, clefted, flamed, mosaic, glass, ceramic, porcelain or quarry, tile is visually rich, transforming everything it touches with its infinite color palette. While the sheer number of tile types is virtually uncatalogued, the variety so diverse, it is always recognized for its solid beauty.

Irridescent irregularly-shaped Tessera tiles, 1" x 1", are face mounted on paper in 11¾" x 11¾" squares.

History in the Making

While it's doubtful that anyone can truly pinpoint the date manmade tile began to be used as an architectural element, there are plenty of clues. Red clay roof tiles, historical scholars assert, appeared on homes in China, 10,000 B.C.; a kiln discovered in Centamura del Chianti in Italy was determined to be of third century B.C. origin. Broken pieces of ceramics were found inside. Beautiful configurations still grace Grecian buildings today, over 2000 years later. But in regard to its development in the United States, we need to look to the 1800s when the first European tile artisans brought their craft with them and began setting up manufacturing facilities. Practices have changed since then, quite obviously, and with those changes, the price of tile has dropped and volume has increased. All good. And yet, with all the dramatic innovations, there are still artisans today who prefer to create their tiles by hand, painting and forming them in small batches, and then firing them in electric kilns.

Tusk colored glazed ceramic tile has a straight edge and is available in three neutral colors including off-white *(shown)*, and light and dark beige.

Today's Tile

Today, employing manmade tile in the interior is widespread. Not just for bathroom or kitchen floors, you will see its beautiful influence on tables, patios, fireplace surrounds, walls—even as accessories, such as trivets, framed art and the requisite mosaic glitter of a 1970s era disco ball. The market is maturing, exhibiting product expansion and more affordable prices. Look for tile that simulates the look of natural stone or wood, new shapes (including a staggering format which offers single pieces as large as three foot by almost four foot), creamy buttery neutrals that offer much more visual interest all while staying within the neutral comfort zone, metallics (copper, gold—and pink) and even "rectified" porcelains, which, because of their entirely straight edges, allow for no grout lines.

Below: This tile's multi-step manufacturing process begins by forming clay from shale that is mined in pits in southeastern Ohio. The natural clay is hand-pressed into flat tiles, trimmed by hand and left to dry for eight hours. A thick coating of clear or colored glaze is hand-applied to ensure durability and long lasting beauty.

The Facts: Tile

Advantages: Color is unaffected by lengthy exposure to light; tiles do not absorb extraneous odors or liquids; tiles do not significantly accrue electrostatic charges, such as you might experience with carpeting, for example; dust, dirt and other residue does not adhere to this type of flooring unless something sticky has been applied first; high resistance to fire. Tile also has a liquid absorption rate of less than five percent; some are as low as 0.5 percent!

Disadvantages: A messier installation process than other flooring materials; grout will stain and/or discolor if not sealed properly; cold to the touch, unless radiant flooring has been installed underneath; can be somewhat loud underfoot; may be slippery when wet; a more dangerous flooring type to fall upon, due to its lack of resiliency; more difficult to repair

Cost: Will depend upon the material, be it glazed or unglazed, glass, porcelain or ceramic.

Lifespan: Centuries

Most Appropriate Locations: Kitchen, bathroom, patio, entryway. Good in areas where moisture may be a problem.

Care & Cleaning: Most often, it is not the tile that needs cleaning as much as it is the grout, as dirt, sand, etc. can be ground into it. As always, sweep often to remove grit from the surface. After that, mop weekly: use one capful of dishwashing liquid in a bucket of water. Buff with a dry towel to reduce spotting; do not use floor wax as it is difficult to remove.

Dream Floors

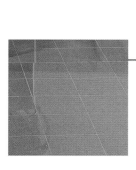

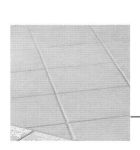

Left: Porcelain tile exhibits realism in depth, color, shade and texture. Blended in a beautiful random mixture within each carton to ensure a gorgeous final installation on both floor and wall, three yummy blends: latte, caramel and macchiato (*shown*) satisfy the tastes of discriminating designers and consumers. Highly resistant to stains and discoloration from virtually any source.

This page, above: A beautiful high polish is just one of the finishes available from this gorgeous line. Varying sizes from 12" x 12" to 3" x 3" offer unlimited possibilities.

This page, below: A soothing bath awaits when you use field tile in pearl gray along with a diamond rug pattern with decorative border. Warm white and beige linen round out the colors available.

Good to Know: Tile

Ceramic Pavers: A result of clay or a mixture of organic materials and pressed into submission rather than extruded, ceramic pavers are finished with a trip to the kiln.

Glass: Think recycled bottles and raw sand, or the tradition of blown glass. Anyway you look at it, glass is a thing of beauty and on the floor, turns into a magnificent work of art. Be sure to select a tile that offers its color fused—rather than painted on—for best results. Non-porous, as durable as marble but infinitely less expensive to acquire and install, glass is known for its clear color beauty and ability to add vibrancy and sparkle to any interior.

Mosaic: An excellent choice for shower stalls. Being the floor needs to be slightly angled toward the drain hole, the small nature of these pieces offers exceptional flexibility in installation. Typically mounted on a backing for ease of installation. Generally made from porcelain or glass.

Porcelain Pavers: This dense tile is made from pressed dust, which results in a finely-grained, velvet-like composition. It is no wonder that beautiful women are said to have complexions "as smooth as porcelain." Available both matte and glazed finishes, porcelain is difficult to cut (making installation a bit more pesky) and is highly water resistant.

Quarry Tile: The most recognizable of the quarry tiles would be those hailing predominantly from the Southwest—terra cotta. Created using an extrusion process incorporating shale or clay, quarry tiles are short on coloration (typically available only in earth tones) and long on performance. Strong and thick, the quarry tile is an excellent choice for hardworking areas where traffic patterns and dirt or moisture collection may be possible. Unglazed tiles tend to last longer than glazed tiles, simply because the glazing will wear thin over time.

Basket gray ½" x ½" tiles form a fascinating pattern. Tiny cubes of powdered colored glass are baked at high temperatures, creating a hardened enamelled finish and an intense purity of color. With an extensive range of 66 colors, it is suitable for both commercial and domestic flooring purposes.
Photo by Alberto Ferrero; project by Fabio Novembre.

Above: Technology and design are continually expanding the decorative qualities of glass. In this beach medallion, clear glass shapes have been sandblasted to an opaque finish, reminiscent of a shard washed smooth by the sea.

Left: Soothing water tones of spruce and midori light up this Seattle, WA bathroom installation designed by Udo Reigh. Photograph by Christopher Ray Photography.

Above: Combining old-world craftsmanship with a modern approach, every piece is meticulously hand-cast, hand-cut and hand-finished. In this New York, NY private bath installation showing glass tile, its homeowners can be assurred that many of the products use up to 85 percent recycled content and begin the manufacturing process as discarded recycled bottle glass. Photograph by Christopher Ray Photography.

Right: The natural beauty of glazed porcelain tile lies in its subtle variation of shades. Please note that some tile (such as the wall tile shown) is not suitable for floor or counter top applications.

Stone Tiles

When it comes to discussing stone, the most primeval of materials, cultural significance cannot be denied. Its very character commands reverence. Eternal, enduring and a true icon of continuity, stone is a bold architectural choice and yet offers the calming grace of nature at its most beautiful.

Written in stone.

Like a rock.

Now and forever, stone as surface material is the penultimate choice for the home that intends to remain for centuries to come.

Considering that the earth is pretty much a big ball of granite, stone tile has been underfoot since, well, the beginning of time. We can trace the beginnings of stone flooring back to about 5000 years ago when walking like an Egyptian meant crossing stone or brick floors, sometimes stopping to admire artistic patterns created, even. Three thousand years ago in Greece, marble was a favorite in tony interiors and temples, characterizing an age of self-indulgence and opulence. Mosaics were also popular, though few could afford them.

Pebbles spread upon a mosque floor in 623 A.D. offered those on bent knees respite from mud after a heavy rain.

Cosmatesque paving, named for the Roman Cosmati family of artisans, was a favorite of the Medieval age, in which colorful marble was cut into small pieces and arranged in geometric designs on the floors.

Indeed, examples could be made throughout the history of the world on how stone flooring enhanced a home environment, making it more beautiful and style resonant. In fact, in an attempt to reconnect with history today, reclaimed stone flooring, harvested from old European farmhouses and chateaus, is available for a pretty penny. Cleaned, recut and catalogued, these lovely granite, flagstone and cobblestone pieces are a terrific way to create a historical look.

Today, the possibilities to blanket the floor with luxurious stone are truly endless. Whether you are choosing a heavily textured slab, be it flamed, sand-blasted or saw-cut, or smooth with a honed or polished finish, you are indeed buying a bit of history, perhaps millions of years old, even.

Polished basketweave tile offers an elongated "brick" pattern available five different color combinations. A 2" x ⅜" bar with ⅜" dot on mesh-mounted .80 square foot sheets, this mosaic pattern is marble. Photo courtesy of Artistic Tile.

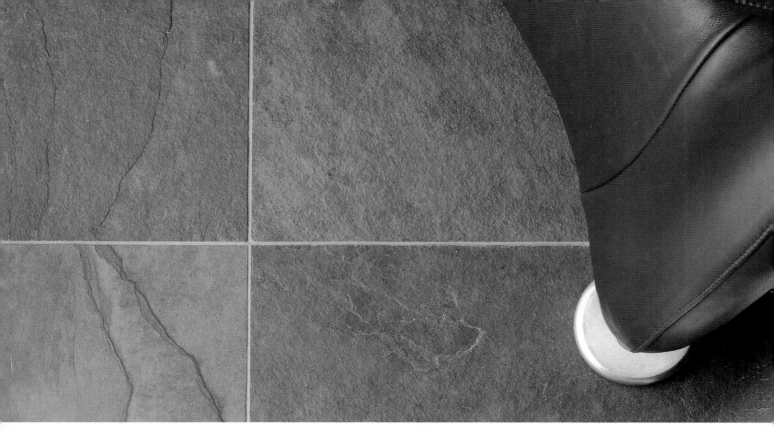

The Facts: Stone Tiles

Advantages: Its diverse patterns, vein streaks and colors, including the possibility of permanently imbedded fossils, offer a unique, naturally beautiful look; cool to the touch—wonderful for a warm climate environment; a connection to the out of doors; sturdy; easy to maintain; extremely durable and perfect for high traffic areas when finished properly

Disadvantages: Even within the same slab, color and vein patterns can vary widely; can be slippery when wet; extremely non-resilient, it can be hard on leg muscles and noisy when trod upon with hard soled shoes; cool to the touch—may need radiant heating in cold weather climates; natural pitting and divoting in stone can capture dirt. Finally, because of its weight, a sturdy subfloor is absolutely necessary.

Cost: Square foot tiles can start as low as $3 to $6; an average range is $12 to $18 per square foot, though expensive finishes and exotic stone can add quite a bit onto the cost. Installation is additional.

Lifespan: Centuries

Most Appropriate Locations: Any room will do; however, entrance halls, kitchens, bathrooms, patios and living rooms grab the lion's share of attention.

Care & Cleaning: Most stone is absorbent (granite being the least) and will stain; caustic cleaners, as well as acidic liquids such as citrus, will etch stone; the best method is to vacuum or sweep and if necessary, clean with non-acidic soap and then rinse with warm water.

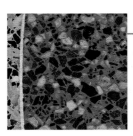

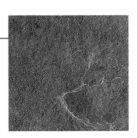

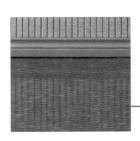

Left: Rio Verde cleft slate is perfect for medium traffic in a variety of stock sizes. This stone offers limited variation in tone; just the deep green beauty of natural slate.

Upper right: Brown terrazzo spiral, from artist Teresa Cox, lends depth and vibrancy to the flat floor surface with its dichotomy of soft and organic linear forms within a hard material.

Lower right: Possibly the most beautiful tile ever, genuine marble chips from around the world are gathered to create 13 traditional and unique colors.

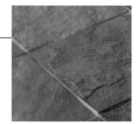

Left: Glorious natural slate in a variety of colors make this floor unbelieveably beautiful. The fireplace also boasts slate, to coordinate well.

Below: A classic form of decoration, mosaic has long been the inspiration for classic design. Here limestone mosaic is accented with contrasting rectangles.

This stone mosaic is surrounded by lagos azul Portuguese stone, available in 4" x 4", 4" x 16", 12" x 12", and 16" x 16" sizes, moldings and mosaics.
Photo courtesy of Artistic Tile.

Good to Know: Stone

How well do you know your rocks?

Granite

An igneous rock—meaning one that was formed by gradually cooling pockets of either magma (below ground) or lava (above ground). Delightfully distinctive, granite contains flecks of mica, quartz and feldspar and thus the colorations are as varied as they are beautiful. Typical colors can range from black and white to browns, yellows, pinks and blues.

The hardest and most resilient of the stones, it is suitable for heavy indoor traffic; most scratches can be buffed out; do not use polished granite if it is to come into contact with water or grease buildup due to slipperiness.

Limestone

A sedimentary rock, meaning one that is formed from the mineral calcite, which is found in evaporated water depositories such as lakes, rivers and seas. It can also be formed from an accumulation of shells or shell fragments.

Frequently, limestone also contains dolomite and aragonite, making this stone typically light in color (tan, gray), although impurities (sand, clay, iron oxides) allow it other variations. It can be finely grained or full of beautiful, rich patterns.

Marble

Polished and highly reflective or honed to a matte finish, you can't beat marble, a sedimentary / metamorphic rock (depending upon whether it is calcinate or dolomitic), in the category of elegance and beauty. Ranging in shades from off white to brown, from gray to green or pink, its surface is hard, but not as hard as granite. Thus, you should be aware that it can scratch and stain easily. Use a honed finish in high volume foot traffic areas; a polished finish should be vertically or in areas that have little traffic.

The clean geometry of this rustic compass medallion makes a bold, elegant statement.

Sandstone

A sedimentary rock, sandstone is comprised of small grains of the quartz and feldspar minerals, which form compressed layers. Varying in color from white to yellow, red, pink, copper and gray, particular colors of sandstone can also be identified as hailing from various regions, such as the red sand of the western United States.

Slate

Hard and dense, laminate-smooth slate is a fine-grained metamorphic rock that is resistant to staining due to its compact composition. Available in a number of color variations including red, gray, black and green, slate absorbs heat rather than reflects it, making it a fine choice for cooler climates. It is also more resilient than other stone products. Must be handled with care upon installation, as it is brittle and splits easily into layers.

Terrazzo

A beautiful mutt, terrazzo is a combination of man-made material (cement or resin) and nature's best. A variety of stone chips, including marble, granite, quartz and onyx are combined and then poured in place or precast, cured, ground and then polished to high luster. Additionally, a rustic terrazzo is available, in which the surface is water washed for a rougher texture.

Travertine

Cousin to limestone, the sedimentary travertine stone ranges in color from light oatmeal to a "coffee with cream" tone, though the colors are rarely standardized. Unique to travertine is the series of cavities and indentations formed by sulfur and gas, which push through the layers when developing. This does create a more intensive cleaning situation, unless a clear epoxy resin has been applied first to create a smooth surface.

.

Above: Although perfect for heavy foot traffic, it may cause a "traffic jam" due to its beautiful looks. Silver/green honed slate will adapt to any situation and any surface. All textured finishes are sound underfoot and will not flake or fade with wear.

Left: When nature bestows her most glorious colors on natural stone, the result is awe inspiring. Exotic stones, such as azul macauba (*shown*), make a bold style statement that transcends time. Photo courtesy of Artistic Tile.

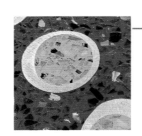

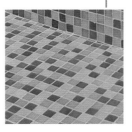

Above: Nothing looks more clean and beautiful than water colors in a bathroom. One inch by one inch tiles in various shades of blue and green, traveling from shower to floor to bathtub are stunning.

Right: Terrazzo artist Teresa Cox began her artistic career in paint before dabbling in terrazzo. She says, "The process of creating in terrazzo, while less direct than painting, is challenging in its myriad of colors, line and aggregate choices. The use of metal line can be a focus or a counterpoint and thus the complexity and layering of material with the image content appears limitless."

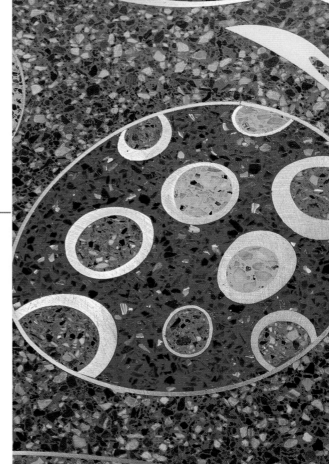

Tile & Stone

Above: The hallmark of this rug mosaic is a warm, creative aesthetic that employs a wealth of color to reinvent any room. This beautiful and versatile collection of colors and shapes offers infinite ways to define a space.

Left: This floor has all the components to enhance the enjoyment of an interior: classically styled listellos and inserts, classic motif listellos sized for both floor and wall, and four field tile sizes in three subtle colors offering delicate visual surface appeal.

Above: A leopard print mosaic prowls across a floor with catlike grace. Design by Carlo Dal Bianco

Right: Rich warm tones of brown and cream tile envelop this shower from top to bottom. Photograph by Christopher Ray Photography.

Above: Glazed porcelain floor tile is a full floor/wall coordinated line in a soft rustic limestone design that duplicates nature.

Right: Warm white and beige linen field tile is a pretty hopscotch of color with subtle, clean looks. When cleaning the grout, use a concentrated household or commercial cleaner (depending on the application). Clean you tile routinely with an all-purpose, non oil-based household or commercial cleaner

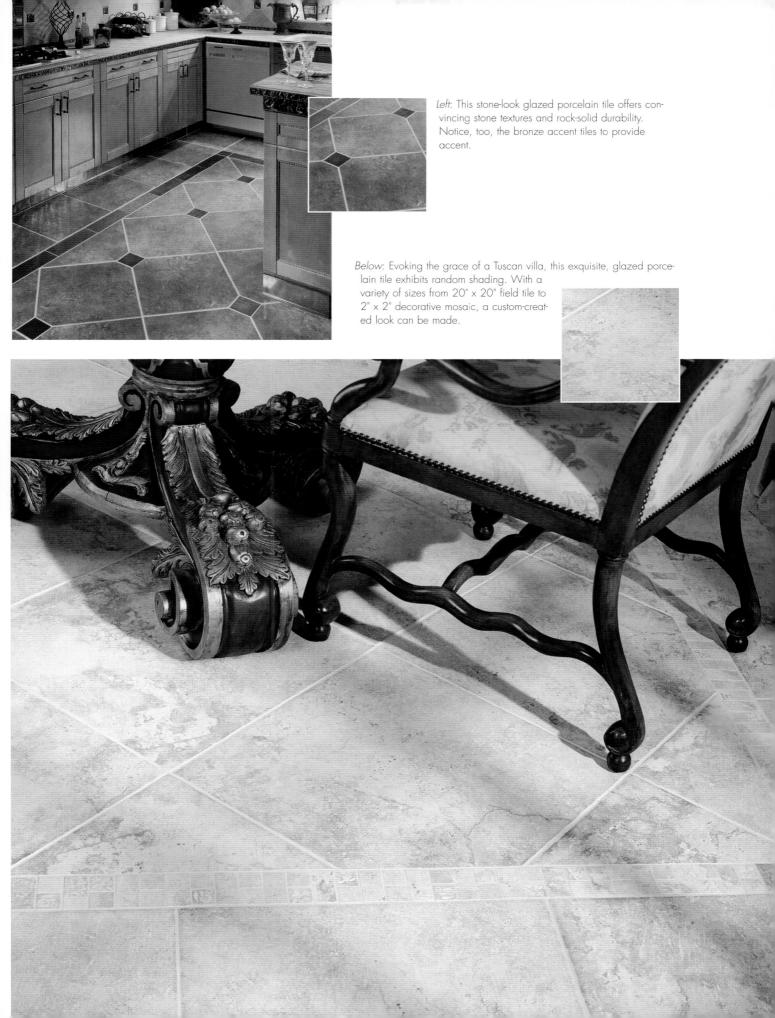

Left: This stone-look glazed porcelain tile offers convincing stone textures and rock-solid durability. Notice, too, the bronze accent tiles to provide accent.

Below: Evoking the grace of a Tuscan villa, this exquisite, glazed porcelain tile exhibits random shading. With a variety of sizes from 20" x 20" field tile to 2" x 2" decorative mosaic, a custom-created look can be made.

Dream Floors

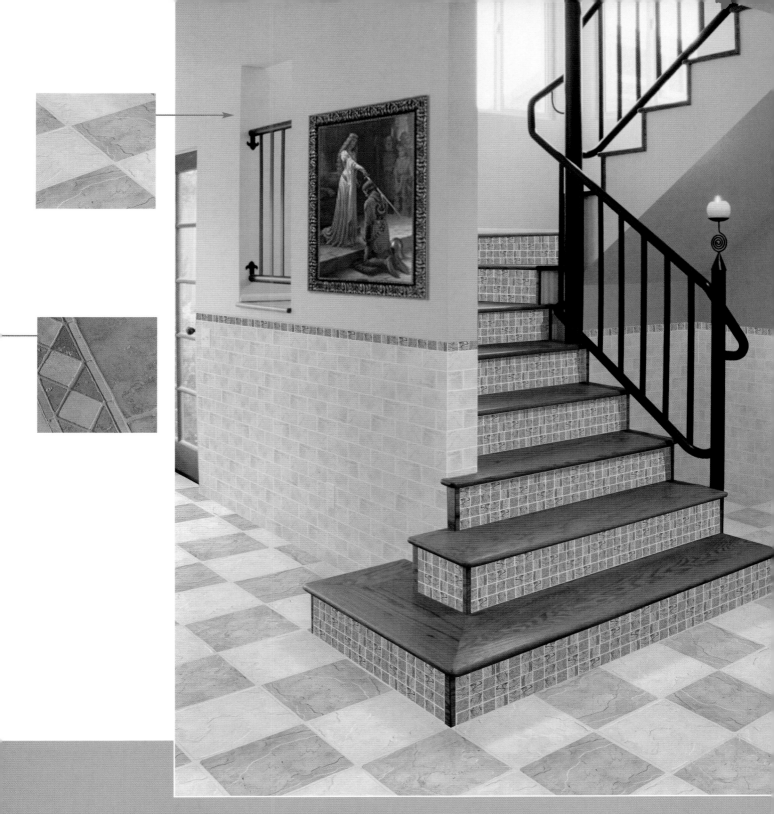

Left: Derived from stone found around the area of Mt. Ararat, this porcelain ceramic tile has a natural stone appeal with all the features and benefits of porcelain ceramic tile. Available in cream, beige and walnut with an optional geometric border, plenty of sophisticated looks can be created.

Above: This dramatically clefted, slatelike floor and wall tile with irregular edges in two generous floor sizes, 13" x 13" and 16" x 16", displays charm and distinction. A mesh-mounted listello made of marble (*see steps*) for additional variety adds dashing individual distinctiveness.

Right: Beautiful colorations: white, sunflower, green, ebony, rust and blue combine to form an exciting array of color and pattern.

Middle: Glazed porcelain floor tiles in a neutral tone are shown here in three different sizes.

Left: This glazed field tile has a warm, complex color palette and an intriguing three-dimensional quality while multiple surface punches and random glaze applications create the look of natural stone.

Dream Floors

Above: For the Via Spiga flagship store in Milano, Italy, gold mosaic ¾" x ¾" glass tile was used, which includes pure 24 karat gold leaf sandwiched between layers of glass. Each tile is entirely handmade.
Photograph by Alberto Ferrero; Fabio Novembre, architect.

Below: Beige floor tiles with a satin finish offer a smooth structure combined with a stone-like pattern.

Above: Eighteen-inch by 18" matte glazed porcelain floor tile is complemented with 4" x 13" scroll bordering and small, four inch square scroll corner pieces.

Below: Porcelain tile can range from charmingly rustic to beautifully elegant. The polished porcelain you see here is available in seven uniquely blended colors that look like authentically honed natural stone. Also available is an embossed border and insert corner, as well as a bullnose trim.

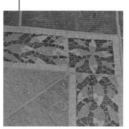

Above: This private residence in Newport Coast, CA, exhibits beautiful limestone field tile. Note the micro-mosaic border—a lovely detail. Photo courtesy of Steve Gunther; design by Dahli deLeon-Brant.

Left: Remarkable striations exhibiting a high degree of color variation run across the weathered, tea stained-like surface of these glazed porcelain tiles. Porcelain tile is very rugged and can withstand much in a variety of interiors and exteriors.

Above: Slate can be tumbled or polished or basically left alone, which results in the beautiful natural cleft slate stone tile. Photo courtesy of Artistic Tile.

Right: Striking beige field tile features the look of antique marble with its pitted surface and subtle shade ranges. Inset detailing is an elegant touch.

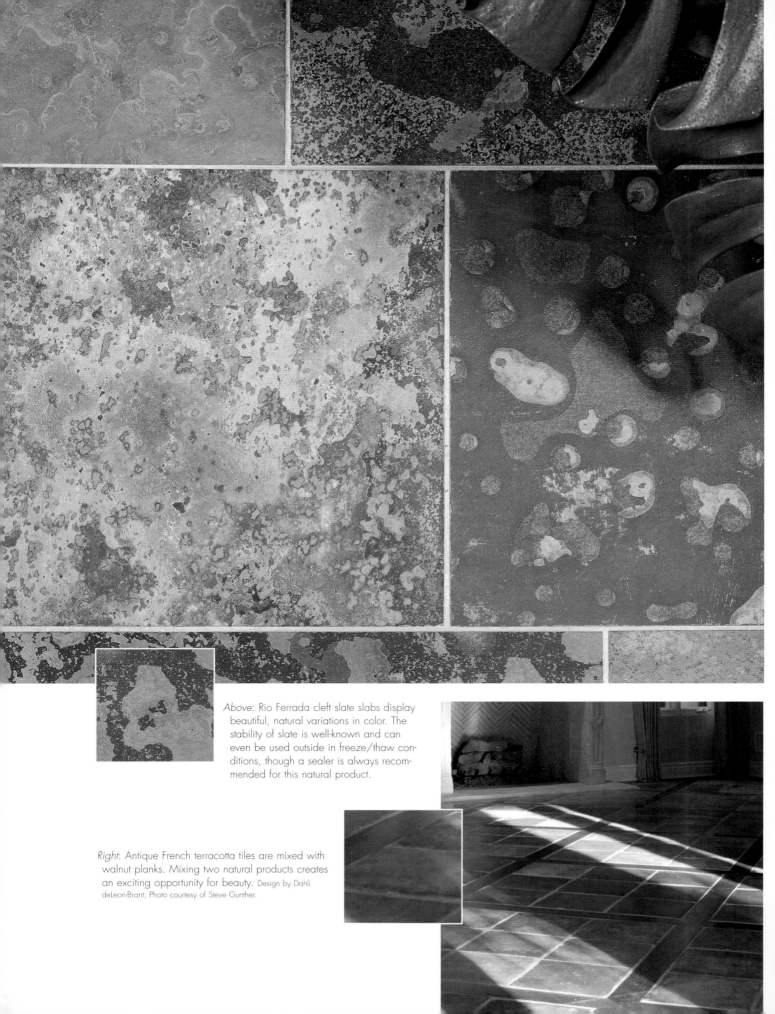

Above: Rio Ferrada cleft slate slabs display beautiful, natural variations in color. The stability of slate is well-known and can even be used outside in freeze/thaw conditions, though a sealer is always recommended for this natural product.

Right: Antique French terracotta tiles are mixed with walnut planks. Mixing two natural products creates an exciting opportunity for beauty. Design by Dahli deLeon-Brant; Photo courtesy of Steve Gunther.

Left: Hot and cool, rich and vibrant, slate, such as this natural cleft herringbone slate makes a visual style statement. Offered in several sizes, finishes and colors from the simple to the startling, slate's complex beauty is derived from its texture and an extreme variation of hues that enriches any room.

Photo courtesy of Artistic Tile.

Below: Artifact relic glazed porcelain floor tile is characterized by its reference to antiquity in both color and design. Its elegant simplicity depicts a warm, time-honored look.

Dream Floors

Left: Breathtaking results can be achieved when ceramic tile is combined with other hard surfaces, such as this lovely tumbled stone mosaic coupled with sandalwood porcelain tile. The wonderful modular nature of tile, the variety of shapes and sizes can provide unlimited possibilities for patterns.

Above: Increasingly familiar in contemporary interiors, limestone has broad appeal. Gentle neutral tones and superior performance are evident in the Nazareth honed limestone, shown above.

Right: In this private residence in Germany, basaltina honed limestone treads, risers and flooring explore the symmetry that exists between steel and glass—and the natural beauty of stone. Photograph courtesy of by Peter Cook.

Middle: Glazed porcelain floor and wall tile in 12" x 12" and 18" x 18" size is suitable for exterior floors and walls in freezing and non-freezing climates when proper installation methods are followed. Application requirements vary for decorative tiles.

Left: Rio Neblina honed slate is perfect for medium foot traffic in common applications—both in and out of doors. A moderate variation in tone throughout its slabs makes it easy on the eye, its coloration so soothing.

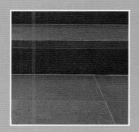

Left: Marble and granite terrazzo tile shows beautiful demarcations and exciting patterning.

Right: A near perfect recreation of natural slate, this porcelain tile is available in a variety of tile sizes to allow creative expression in patterning.

Left: Suede limestone has deep chocolate and olive tones and rich, beautiful veining. The surface texture is extremely smooth and feels wonderful underfoot. This stone is at once elegant, warm and inviting.

Right: Mosaic medallions can be a striking punctuation of soft curves and gentle lines. This Pietre Romane medallion, 60" x 60" is surrounded by Gascogne beige honed limestone.

Above: Slate-look tiles are as rugged as all outdoors. Porcelain stone tile can take a beating both indoors and out. Harder than natural stone (30 percent harder than marble, for example), high-fire porcelain tile is virtually impervious to moisture, so it shrugs off the freeze/thaw winter conditions that can reduce lesser tiles to rubble.

Left: Glazed porcelain floor tile is good for heavy residential applications. Pair it with contour edging to set off a distinct area within your living space.

Above: An innovative manufacturing process and glazing technique produces truly unique tiles with edges that appear to have been worn soft by the passage of time. In an ancient art form known as "rubblework," shards of all six colors are tumbled to gentle their sharp edges, creating the dramatic texture of this border.

Right: Rustic beauty with an elegant touch. Designed for heavy usage, its texture, shading and color variations create a convincing stone appearance. Available in six colors, each tile is a unique blending of several hues.

A porcelain product that resembles the natural beauty of slate, this tile is a brillant imposter. The enchantment of this product is that it is actually durable, frost-resistant, glazed porcelain tile from Italy, with all of the rich colorations and variations of natural slate.

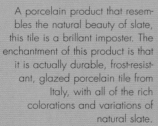

Creating a space within a space makes tile flooring infinitely interesting. Note how by placing the tile squares at an alternate angle and emphasizing them with a detailed border creates the look of a rug.

Retro black and white tile combinations take a person back in time and forward into home fashion. Checkerboard marble decoratives and classic black and white octagons for floors are a standout for the classic interior.

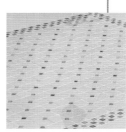

Enjoy all of the natural beauty of travertine stone without the high maintenance and cost. A slightly textured surface with tone-on-tone detail and subtle, muted color palette will work easily with today's interiors.

Left: Enjoy the beauty and grace of these field tiles, with the soft tone-on-tone shading of natural stone and lovely bamboo leaf border detailing.

Above: Named after the Greek God of eternal beauty, Endymion porcelain is a dynamic tile that captures the essence of the Mediterranean in an array of sun drenched, neutral tones. A durable but beautiful tile, it will work well in areas of medium to high traffic.

Above: Warm, coffee colored stone with side set square accents and narrow border make for a relaxing environment. Photo courtesy of Lowitz and Company.

Left: A contemporary sandstone application, every stone from is hand picked and sorted by color, size and thickness, then hand puzzled together to create a tile that is unique and uniform.

Above: Bronze liners create a cross-rhythm with Indian slate tiles—an exciting change from using all grout.

Right: Beige field tile in a 12" x 12" diamond pattern set off the matching 8" x 8" fireplace surround and mantel.

Dream Floors

Left: A luxurious bathroom retreat is set apart by the unique application of small and large tiles in a circular pattern.

Middle: The realistic look of randomly colored slate is combined with the durability of porcelain stone. Perfect for indoor and outdoor flooring applications, this product can extend from your kitchen, right through the French doors and out onto your patio. Available in two different finishes: a slip-resistant outdoor surface and a smooth, easy-to-clean indoor surface.

Right: This blend of urban metal and concrete looks is all done up in porcelain. Generously sized tiles of 13" x 13" and 20" x 20" are available in three colors, urban gray, skyline silver and midtown bronze—a most sophisticated look.

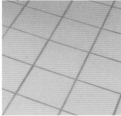

Above: Quarry tile production has its roots in the brick making industry and uses raw material very similar to that used
in the manufacture of brick products. These tiles, however,
are not produced in a quarry, they are manufactured. High
quality quarry tiles are made from a mixture of natural
ingredients including clays and shales, extruded and then
fired at a high temperature.

Left: This tile is a "through body" porcelain tile which has
been slightly glazed to obtain its unique appearance.
Through body means the color and pigment that created this
look extends throughout the body of the tile.

Right: Rustic 13" x 13" tile with coordinating decorative
corner/insert is a delight.

Alternatives

HOW MUCH DO YOU CARE ABOUT RESALE VALUE OF YOUR HOME? Have you always wanted to try something different on your floors but were afraid that it would impact the resale value of your home in a negative way? Rest assured, the new alternatives are making strong headway in "cool factor" and many of the new flooring materials are strong sellers. Consider not just concrete—but colored, acid washed concrete. Think about leather—it's gorgeous! What about metal? Brick? These are just some of the wonderful and creative materials to wrap your head around today. Here's a look.

Bordeaux-colored leather tile, in a 6" x 12" offset brick pattern is warm and resilient, and hand-polished to a rich luster. This fashion statement today is a classic for tomorrow. Photo courtesy of Artistic Tile.

Good to Know: Alternatives

A quick tutorial on the many alternative flooring products available today.

Acid Stained Concrete

This isn't your standard garage floor. Acid stained concrete is a relatively new fad that can transform both old and new floors into works of art. But this finishing technique isn't, as the name implies, brought about by acid, but through a reaction of an application of acidic salts to the surface to the concrete. Concrete contains calcium hydroxide, and it is this substance the salts latch onto, creating colors such as black, brown and blue-green.

- Advantages: Can transform an existing concrete floor from blah to beautiful and not compromise its structural integrity; no worries about destroying/protecting the floor—after all, it's concrete!

- Disadvantages: New concrete must be allowed to settle for at least one month prior to staining. Old concrete must be completely free of dirt, oil and other pollutants. Moisture content needs to be below twelve percent in order for the stain to be effective.

Reactive stains are unique to each concrete surface they are applied to and will produce a wide range of variation depending on many factors, including but not limited to, finishing techniques, mix designs, curing practices, age and condition of existing slab, base color, and surface porosity. Wide variations, mottling and unevenness of color should be expected and are desired. This private residence in Newport Beach, CA shows beautiful earthy variations of color. Design by Dahli deLeon-Brant; Photo courtesy of Steve Gunther.

Leather

Installed and similar in many ways to ceramic tile, leather offers an inimitable statement in any room. Unlike your jacket or your favorite pair of shoes, this leather has been specially processed through dying and tanning that makes it hard to the touch, yet is warm and supple underfoot. A great contemporary look, leather will complement any wood motif.

• Advantages: Exceptional sound absorption; tile color extends through the entire piece. Should it be cut or opened up in any way, the same color would show; a very unique, contemporary look.

• Disadvantages: Expensive; susceptible to heat, salt

Historic brickwork. Designer Wendy Richens, Richens Designs Inc., elaborates about the house and its floor, "it was an original hunting lodge in the Benedict Canyon area of Beverly Hills. The brick flooring (*shown below*) was originally the exterior flooring. I guess when they decided to enlarge the lodge and add the kitchen they just built right over the brick and it became the kitchen floor. The pattern continues outside. When I came in to redesign the kitchen, I looked down and said 'we have to use the floor!' So I designed the kitchen around the floor!"

and bleach; water resistancy is low; tiles are not "perfect"—i.e., care needs to be taken when fitting them next to one another on the floor.

Metal

Uniquely surface-refined to reflect light and color, metal tiles can create a beautiful shimmer, providing stellar animation from every view.

- Advantages: Highly moisture resistant, metal tiles can be used anywhere wet or dry, indoors or out. Metal tiles, especially those made of bronze, will develop a beautiful patina after exposure to water and other elements, ranging from a soft green, to blue hues or even an opaque tone. If you prefer to keep your tiles in pristine condition, you can polish them with a soft abrasive pad or even use something such as copper cleaner.
- Disadvantages: Some metal tiles are made of pewter and can scratch and gouge easily. This also holds true for plated tiles, and those made of metal composites that have been wrapped

around a non-metal core layer. Make certain you buy a tile that will hold up in the conditions you are accustomed to.

Floorcloths

Basically, a painting for your floor, floor cloths are an art form that spans centuries. Heavy canvases, such as discarded ship sails, were used to cover floors. But as many may understand, a blank canvas begs to be painted. From this, floor cloth paintings resulted. Although popular up until linoleum grabbed the spotlight, floorcloths are making a comeback today due to their emphasis on flexibility and durability.

Note that the final artwork should be protected with a clear matte acrylic sealer in order to keep the it protected from surface dirt, oils and ultraviolet rays.

- Advantages: Heavy duty, durable and easy to maintain, floorcloths are vibrant and beautiful expressions of an artist's vision. You should be

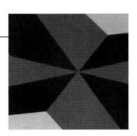

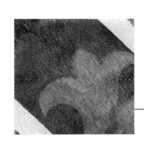

Left: Perfect for areas prone to muddy feet and spills, floor cloths are sturdy and can take a beating. The background is a faux finish using a light and a darker cream shade with a brownish red border.

Above: Bronze sunrise tiles are set with limestone and travertine marble mosaic to create a most unusual and lovely floor. Each metal tile is first carved by hand in sculptor's wax. From these original wax tiles multiple casts are made. At the foundry, these patterns are pressed into specially prepared, fine, moist sand. The patterns are carefully removed, leaving exact impressions of the designs in the sand. Then, into each cavity the studio pours white-hot molten bronze. Beauty ensues. Photo courtesy of Lowitz & Company.

Below: Shown are 4" x 4' metal planks with 4" metal Alpha Blue accent tiles—truly unique!

able to clean your cloth with a simple liquid cleanser. A moveable floor covering, you can take it with you when you move—or gift it and leave it for future generations to enjoy—just ask Thomas Jefferson. He presented a green canvas floorcloth to the White House, which still lies there today in what is now known as the "Green Room."

• Disadvantages: Good floorcloths take some time to create, as each layer of paint needs to dry completely before the next layer is applied. Count on waiting at least four to six weeks for a good cloth. Poorly-constructed floor cloths will roll and curl at the edges. Make certain your floorcloth has been created on heavy canvas stretched tight and primed with eight to ten layers of paint. This way, your floorcloth will lie perfectly flat on your floor.

Brick

Not just for exterior applications anymore, brick makes a strong statement in any home where alternative floor coverings are welcome. Unmatched for its combination of durability and character, new brick, as well as recycled brick, is making headway in today's upscale interiors, as well as rustic retreats.

• Advantages: Brick is great in areas of heavy traffic; capable of withstanding extreme temperature changes. Slip resistant—even when wet; a warm, natural look; color extends throughout the entire piece.

• Disadvantages: Colorations are relatively traditional. A sturdy subfloor is absolutely necessary, due to the weight of this product, although thin brick pavers are less heavy than construction-style bricks.

Dream Floors

Left: This solid aluminum metal tile is handmade by artisans from start to finish. The artist begins with a solid piece of ⅜" aluminum which is cut into tile size pieces. Every tile is uniquely surface refined to reflect light and color the way only metal can, creating a beautiful shimmer that animates the tile from every view. The color and patterns are then hand applied. Because all tile is handmade, each piece is as unique a creation as an original painting.

Middle: Floor cloth artist Tracy Whelan uses multiple layers of water based paint to create her floorcloths and also miters and hems the edges so the floorcloth lies flat. It is varnished with three coats of polyacrylic varnish for ease of cleaning and durability. She says, "when cleaning in my kitchen I typically don't even move the floorcloth, I just vacuum and mop right over it." *Shown above:* The tan and red floorcloth design was taken from a floor stencil from the Edward Durant House in Newton, MA. The house was built circa 1734 with the stenciling done around 1780.

Right: Metal accent tiles are available in a variety of sizes, including 2½" x 2½", 4" x 4" and 6" x 6".

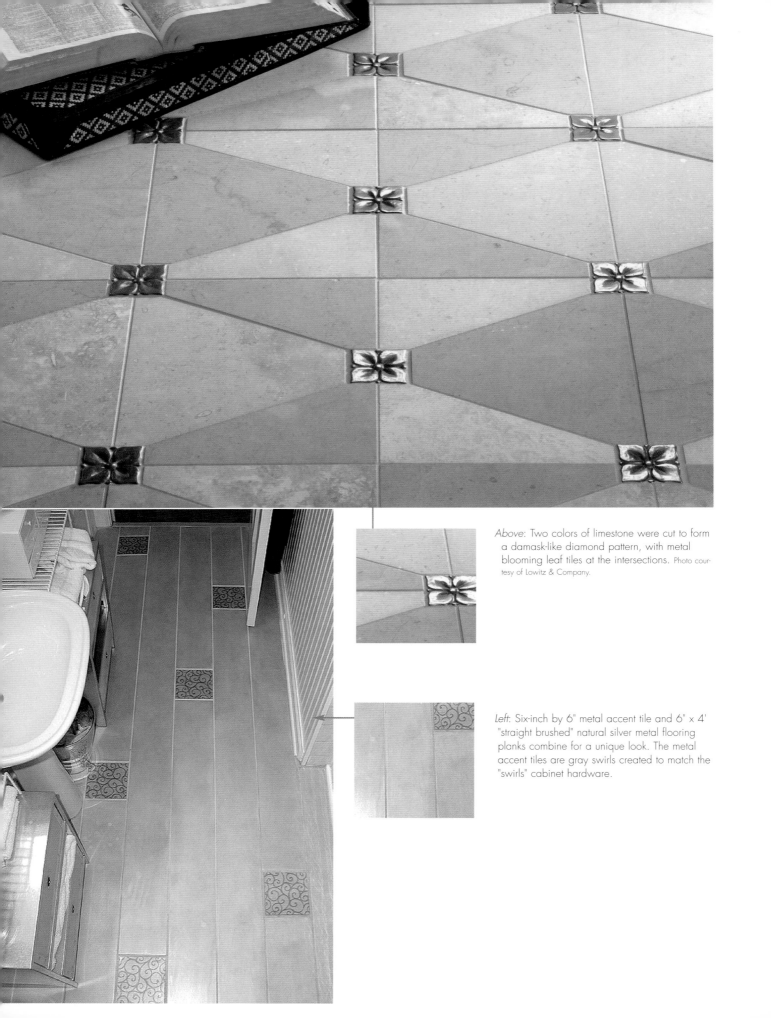

Above: Two colors of limestone were cut to form a damask-like diamond pattern, with metal blooming leaf tiles at the intersections. Photo courtesy of Lowitz & Company.

Left: Six-inch by 6" metal accent tile and 6" x 4' "straight brushed" natural silver metal flooring planks combine for a unique look. The metal accent tiles are gray swirls created to match the "swirls" cabinet hardware.

Above: Ruffles accent tiles define a pattern within a pattern in this basketweave marble floor. Each tile, prior to release, is brushed with a protective coat of wax to slow down the natural patina process. Finally, with a soft cloth, the tiles are hand-polished. Photo courtesy of Lowitz & Company.

Right: Concrete artist Sylvia Beez sees interior design as a 3-D art form. A unique design, representing an abstract landscape, materialized on a concrete floor in this installation. The floor was first scored into a mosaic of shapes. Then each shape was stained individually with a faux finish technique, applying multiple layers of colored stain. The result is a highly individualized floor solution for those who are looking for something special.

Alternative Flooring

Left: Interior designer Edward Stough, ASID, used leather floor tiles to warm this cozy den. Photo courtesy of Ron Solomon.

Above: Resurfaced concrete will give your driveway an absolute new look. By resurfacing existing concrete in garages, walkways, patios, pool areas and driveways, A completely new look can be created without the unnecessary noise, dust and expense of breaking and removing existing concrete.

Almost anything can be considered alternate—this vinyl flooring looks like vibrant ceramic tile, enhancing a beautifully modern bathroom.

Glossary

A

Above-grade: Meaning that the floor itself is not touching the ground and also has at least eighteen inches of well-ventilated space between.

Abrasion resistance: The degree to which a flooring surface will be able to withstand foot traffic and other wear-and-tear. There are six classified degrees, which range from decorative use to light, medium, heavy and extra heavy residential and commercial applications.

Abrasive finish: A non-reflective, flat surface finish.

Abstract: A pattern or design not based on normal design theories.

Acanthus: A motif based on the acanthus leaf. The design originated in Greece, where it was used on the capitals of the Corinthian columns.

Acclimation: A period of time where flooring materials are stored in the area of installation for equalization of moisture content/humidity levels. Laminate flooring, for example, should be acclimated for about 48 hours prior to install. Not required for all flooring types.

Acoustical properties: How a flooring reacts to various sound waves by absorbing, reflecting or transmitting.

Adhesive: A substance that joins two materials, typically dissimilar, together. An example would be resilient flooring to a subfloor.

Agate: Quartz, a stone, typically showing colored bands or other markings.

Agglomerated product: A stone product, manmade, that consists primarily of crushed stone such as marble, granite and quartz. These chips are mixed with resins and natural pigments and then made available in a variety of sizes, from small tiles to large slabs.

Ambering: A temporary visual yellowing occurring in linoleum flooring that will disappear (and not reappear) when exposed to sunlight. To test, cover half of one piece with cardboard and put in direct sunlight for one hour. Remove the covering and you will immediately see the change. Also called "Blooming."

Annual growth rings: Each ring is a marker of one full year of wood growth. This circular pattern (seen in cross-section) is not only beautiful, but can also provide a close approximation of the age of the tree.

Antimicrobial: A chemical treatment that helps diminish the growth of common household bacteria such as mold, mildew and yeast. Typically built into the product such as in the carpet cushion, between the wear layers of laminate, etc.

Antistatic: An electrostatic charge is dissipated within the flooring, in particular carpet and rugs, before it reaches a threshold a human can feel.

Arabesque: A pattern or style that uses flowers, foliage, fruit or sometimes animal and human figures to produce an intricate pattern of interlaced lines.

Art Deco: A design style from the 1920s and 1930s that emphasizes rounded, stylized motifs.

Art Nouveau: This "new art" style focuses on swirling lines, such as plant stems and tendrils.

Attached cushion: A material, such as foam, PVC, rubber, etc. that is attached to the underside of the carpet to enhance strength, thickness and padding.

Aubusson rug: The name hails from Aubusson, France, a mid-17th century production center. The first Aubusson designs were based on Turkish models but later 19th century rugs took on an English slant. Tapestry, typically portraying flowers, bouquets and architectural themes.

Axminster carpet: This machine-woven carpet offers colorful patterns in a wide variety of colors.

B

Backing: The underside of the carpet that touches the sub floor. There are different kinds: In tufted carpet, for example, a primary backing is a fabric, either woven or non-woven, that the carpet yarn is inserted through by way of tufting needles. A secondary backing is one in which fabric is laminated onto the back of the carpet fibers to reinforce and provide stability. In woven carpet, the backing is a yarn that is interwoven from behind to stabilize the face yarn.

Baseboard: A decorative board that is placed at the bottom of the wall next to the floor to conceal joints and offer a finished appearance.

Basket-weave pattern: Flooring that imitates the tightly or loosely woven construction of a basket. Can be done in many types of materials including stone, tile and resilient materials.

Bed: Can refer to either a natural bed of rock or also to a layer of binding adhesive covering a surface that is to be tiled.

Below-grade: Meaning that the finished floor is in direct contact with the ground or has less than 18 inches of well-ventilated space. Usually a basement floor.

Berber: A loop pile carpet (*see* loop pile) with a base color, coupled with random flecks of contrasting hues. Informal and casual, it is hard wearing and available in a variety of loop sizes, from small and flat to large and nubby.

Binding: A band, stitch or strip of fabric sewn along the edge of a carpet or rug to keep it from unraveling or fraying and/or to decorate it.

Bird's Eye: Small, circular areas on the surface of wood (primarily maple) that resemble the eyes of birds but are actually indented fibers.

Bisque: A mixture of clay, water and other additives that have been shaped into tile.

Blemish: A defect, typically found in a natural flooring such as wood, that spoils its appearance.

Blooming: *see* Ambering

Borders: A decorative strip of flooring that can be used abutting the molding, around doors or to delineate areas within a room. Borders often correspond with the main flooring type and/or color.

Bow: When a wood plank or strip has curvature from one end to the other. Horns Up bowing is when the ends point toward the ceiling; Horns Down refers to the strip or plank pointing downward.

Braided: Rugs crafted from thick strips of yarn or fabric that have been braided into dense ropes. The braids are then stitched side-to-side in a variety of circular patterns, creating a reversible rug.

Breaking strength: A flooring's ability, particularly tile, to withstand weight loads. A minimum strength required is 250 pounds.

Broadloom: Typically applies to carpet produced in widths wider than six feet. Most often, broadloom is twelve feet wide but can also be found in six, thirteen-and-a-half and fifteen-foot widths.

Broom finish: Sweeping a broom over fresh concrete to add surface texture.

Brush finish: Using a coarse wire brush on stone to rough up a finish.

Bull nose: A convex trim tile used for finishing; typically a stair tread or an outside corner.

Burl: A swirl or twist within the wood grain that is usually found near a knot. A beautiful, natural mark.

C

Cable: Cut pile construction carpeting with long pile height and casual, chunky tufts.

Carpet backing: *see* Backing

Carpet pile: Fibers forming the surface of carpet.

Carpet tile: Primarily for heavy commercial usage, carpet tiles are large, durable squares backed with vinyl.

Ceramic tile: Typically mosaic or quarry, this tile is made from clay or a mixture of natural, organic materials, and then finished in a kiln.

Chalk line: A cord coated with chalk is pulled tightly and then snapped quickly onto the floor to establish a horizontal plumb line, so as to properly align tile squares, for example.

Cleavage: A natural cleft within a stone that may cause a stone to crack, break or delaminate.

Cloudy: A loss of luster or a milky appearance on the surface finish.

Colorfastness: A material's capacity to resist color change when exposed to sunlight and various liquids.

Composite: A concealed unit onto which a stone is permanently bonded to provide stability and/or to anchor the stone in place.

Concrete: Sand, gravel and water mixed with portland cement. May also be confused with the word, cement.

Continuous Pressure Laminate (CPI): Laminate's multiple layers are fused together under heat and pressure to form a single unit; then, in a separate process, they are again subjected to heat and pressure, along with glue, and bonded to a core board.

Core: The inner portion of an engineered board, such as layers two through four in a six-layer product.

Cork flooring: Harvested from the bark of the cork oak

tree in a sustainable manner, cork is a replenishable, resilient flooring material available in both tile, sheet good and plank form.

Cushion: A material placed under a carpet to enhance softness underfoot, provide enhanced acoustical and insulation benefits and also longer wear life. Can also be called "padding," "underlay" or "lining." Is occasionally attached directly to the carpet at the time of manufacture. Should be no thicker than ⅜".

Cut and loop pile: A combination of both intact loops and cut loops, offering the possibility for plenty of surface textures, including sculptured effects, swirls, squares and more.

Cut pile: Yarn loops are cut, creating texture and a welcoming feel underfoot. Hides foot and vacuum cleaner marks. Most well known as "Shag," cut pile loop was, and still is, one of the most popular carpet types.

D

Décor layer: The second layer in the composition of laminate flooring's four layers. Also known as the "beauty" layer, as it is this sheet that provides the visual aesthetics.

Delamination: Can refer to many different flooring types. In essence, it is the separation of one layer from another, such as the secondary backing separating from the primary backing of a piece of carpet or the failure of a bond between the adhesive in an engineered board and its veneer.

Density: The amount of pile yarn or fiber within a carpet and how close together they are. Typically, the more yarn, the denser the pile, thus better performance is achieved.

Dimensional stability: The ability of a floor to maintain its original shape over its lifetime, factoring in changes in humidity, climate and traffic patterns.

Direct Pressure Laminate (DPL): (*also* Direct Laminate Process) A laminating process in which a single press is employed to fuse the finish layers and backing layers to the core board.

Directional print: A pattern designed with the specific intention of being installed in a certain direction to achieve the desired effect.

Distressing: (*also* Distressed) The act of gouging, scraping, scratching or in other ways artificially texturing a floor covering to impart a time worn appearance.

Dhurrie: Usually constructed of cotton or wool, this flat-woven rug hails from India.

Double glue-down: An installation procedure for carpeting in which the padding is first adhered to the subfloor with adhesive, then the carpet is glued to the padding.

Drugget: Usually constructed of goat hair, cotton and/or jute, this non-pile rug hails from India and the Balkans.

E

Eclectic: An inclusion of many different styles from different places and periods.

Efflorescence: A residue resembling a whitish powder or crust that sometimes appears on the surface of unglazed tiles, brick, concrete and similar materials. It is caused by moisture reacting with impurities in the mortar. There are a number of products on the market today to remove efflorescence and then seal the stone.

Embossed-in-Register: First patented by Faus Group Inc. in 2000. A process designed to bring an authentic look and feel of natural wood, ceramic and stone to laminate flooring products.

Embossing: Deliberate texturing (high and low areas) in stone, carpet and other flooring materials for functional and aesthetic reasons.

Engineered wood flooring: Likened to high-end plywood, engineered wood flooring is comprised of three to seven layers of wood veneer, aligned at 90 degrees to the one beneath it. This layering provides exceptional dimensional stability—it will shrink and swell less than solid hardwood.

F

Face: The exposed portion of stone flooring, in particular.

Field stone: Blocks that have separated from larger rocks or ledges through natural processes and have been scattered across the soil cover.

Figure: Referring to wood. The imperfections, markings and configurations made by nature's elements during the natural growth of a tree.

Fire resistance: The ability of a floor covering to withstand fire or to provide protection from it.

Fire retardant: A chemical used on a floor covering to retard the spread of fire over that surface.

Flagstone: Fine-grained sandstone, slate, etc. used in thin slabs for paving patios, walks and driveways.

Fleur-de-lis: The fleur-de-lis was a stylized iris flower adopted by French kings as a royal symbol.

Floating floor: A floor not attached directly to the floor or subfloor (thus, "floating"), but connected together. Can be installed over an existing floor.

Fluffing: Loose fiber fragments on a carpet surface left after installation. Remedy by vacuuming. Should not appear again, although is occasional after wet cleaning. Also called "shedding" or "fuzzing."

Fluting: Parallel, carved depressions in wood or stone that imitate a long groove.

Focal point: The major point of interest in a room, such as a fireplace.

Frieze: Pronounced *free-zay*, this tightly curled cut pile masks vacuum cleaner marks and footprints. Superior texture retention due to the tight twist.

Fur: Natural fur rugs, such as combed sheepskin, are lush and luxurious. Alpaca, for example, is sheared from an animal; hide rugs (such as cowhide) are culled from those animals discarded by the food industry or from natural circumstances.

G

Gabbeh: Coarse rugs adorned with abstract patterns and native images. Originally attributed to the nomads of Iran's central Zagros Mountains, who used them in tents. Recently recognized for their artistic value.

Gauge: The distance between two needlepoints in a knitted or tufted carpet, measured in fractions of an inch.

Glass tile: Tiles made of glass, usually mounted on 12" x 12" sheets of paper.

Glaze: A ceramic coating fired to a glassy state, used to cover clay tiles. There are a number of different glazes including those with and without color; those containing microscopic crystals or contrasting granules of color; low gloss; high gloss; semi-transparent and more.

Glazed tile: Fire-hardened clay tiles covered with a moisture resistant matte or glossy glaze and sealant.

Gloss level: Gloss can be highly reflective or a low shine. A gloss level is measured by a glossometer and offers up a number from 0 to 100, with 100 being mirror-like and 0 being black.

Grade levels: There are three: below grade (below the ground level), grade (at the ground) and above grade (above ground level).

Granite: A very hard, igneous rock consisting of feldspar, quartz and other minerals. Granite is very resistant to damage, but requires some periodic care.

Grout: A pouring consistency mixed-mortar. Whether the grout being used is fine or course depends upon the size of the grout space being used.

Growth ring: *see* Annual growth ring

H

Hand: How a carpet feels when a hand is run over its surface.

Hand-hooked (Hand-tufted): A rug-making process in which yarn is inserted into a pattern-stenciled backing material with a hand-held tufting tool. After the hooking is complete, a second backing is attached to anchor and protect the stitches.

Hand-knotted: Pile yarns are knotted around warp fibers that run the length of the rug. The more knots each square inch holds, the more valuable the rug.

Hardwood: Surprisingly, this term does not infer hardness in its physical sense but instead refers to broad-leafed or deciduous trees versus softwood, which comes from needle-bearing and coniferous trees.

Harlequin: Diamond shapes arranged into different patterns.

Heat setting: A heat or steam process that sets a yarn's twist, enabling it to hold that twist over time and bounce back with good resilience.

High Pressure Laminate: A two-step process of heat and pressure, coupled with glue, bonding the core laminate material layers with the finish and back layers.

I

Impact resistance: The ability of a flooring material, in particular ceramic tile and stone, to resist breakage or surface chipping. Typically, unglazed tiles are less susceptible to surface chipping than glazed tiles.

Inserts: Usually a small, decorative tile used in conjunction with a larger, plain tile to create an accent or pattern.

If it is small and square, it is called an inset.

Inset: *see* Inserts

Iridescent: Typically seen in tiles with a lustrous glaze that contains, seemingly, a variety of changing colors.

J

Jute: A soft, shiny fiber that can be spun into coarse threads. In turn, these threads can become rope—or crafted into a rug. Inexpensive.

K

Kilim: A flat-woven rug with pileless, smooth surfaced weaving.

Knot hole: An opening created when a knot falls from the wood in which it was initially embedded.

KPSI: Knots per square inch

L

Laminate flooring: Developed in Sweden in the mid-1970s, laminate consists of four layers (wear, beauty, fiberboard and back), which can resemble just about any type of wood or tile. Inexpensive and perfect for high traffic households. Available in planks or squares.

Lava: An igneous rock; one that has erupted from the earth due to volcanic action.

Level loop pile: Stitched in level, uncut loops of the same height and size, this informal carpet is very suitable for high-traffic areas. The popular flecked Berber carpet is one example. May be woven or tufted.

Limestone: A very porous, sedimentary rock consisting mainly of calcium carbonate. Compact, dense and capable of taking a polish.

Linoleum flooring: Introduced in the 1800s, resilient linoleum was wildly popular in the 1950s until vinyl flooring took over in popularity. Recently experiencing a new trend surge due to its environmentally-friendly, 100 percent biodegradable nature, as well as antistatic, hypoallergenic qualities.

M

Mahal: A rug of medium weave and knot count with a cotton foundation. The name most likely refers to the region of Mahallat. Although of average quality, the design and soft color combination, along with its smooth hand and lustrous wool elevates its price.

Marble: A metamorphic rock formed from limestone that is very common in architecture and sculpture. Elegant appearance. Can be highly polished.

Matte finish: A dull finish.

Mexican paver tile: A handmade tile that can vary in texture, size and shape. Typically coated with a glaze to provide a wear surface.

Mission: This style is based upon the Southern California Spanish missions, and the southwestern flair they contain.

Mixed media flooring: Flooring of predominantly one type but also incorporating other materials as contrast, such as a wood floor with tile borders.

Monochromatic: One color, or possibly different tones of one color.

Monocottura: A glazed or unglazed tile produced by a single firing.

Mosaic: A type of flooring that uses small pieces of glass, stone and tile set in cement to form a pattern. Typically, the stone is of an irregular shape and size.

Multi-level loop pile: Two or three various uncut loop heights create patterns, hide stains and offer a casual carpeted look.

Mural: A mural is a large pictorial design that often covers an entire floor. Marble or ceramic tile are typical materials.

N

Natural cleft: *see* Cleavage

Needlepoint: Wool yarn is worked onto a pattern-stenciled canvas in the same way that, for example, a needlepoint pillow is made. Hand-sewn.

O

Obsidian: Lava in its glassy phase.

Oriental rug: A hand-woven or hand-knotted rug indigenous to the Middle or Far East.

Outside corner: A corner formed when two walls, not facing each other, are joined.

Vibrant color changes are part of the allure of linoleum, a product once at its height in the 1950s, now experiencing a resurgence due to its environmentally-friendly properties.

Dream Floors

P

Painted: The application of paint to a rug or canvas. Sealer is placed over the top to protect this fragile medium.

Paisley: Paisley is a comma-shaped motif named after the town of its origin, Paisley, Scotland.

Parquet: Small slats of wood are assembled into individual decorative or patterned squares and then installed onto the subfloor.

Persian: Rugs named for the primary carpet weaving areas of Iran (formerly Persia). Typically comprised of a rich, beautiful wool or silk with curvilinear floral designs. Graceful and intricate, their delicate tones are not only beautiful, but perfectly coordinated.

Pickled floor: White paint is rubbed into a stained, finished wood floor to provide an informal, casual look.

Pile: Referring to the visible surface of carpeting. Also "face" or "nap."

Pile crush: When carpet tufts are crushed beyond their capacity to rebound. Typically due to compression by heavy furniture. To combat, vacuum frequently and adjust furniture.

Pilling: When tufts of carpet tangle together and form hard fiber masses. Remove the fibers carefully by trimming with scissors.

Plaid: Designs consisting of crossed stripes, many of them originating in Scottish tartans.

Plain sawn: When lumber is culled at a parallel angle, displaying the grain patterns and growth rings most.

Plank flooring: Wood flooring that is typically about three to eight inches wide, about five or six times longer than wide and installed in parallel rows.

Plush: Velvety in appearance due to fibers cut to the same length, this carpet is demanding in its appearance, showing vacuum cleaner marks at will. Luxurious to the touch and beautiful, there is no better smooth surface in carpeting. Individual tufts are not visible.

Ply: Relates to the single fiber in a yarn. Thus, a two-ply yarn would tell you that two single fibers have been twisted together, etc.

Porcelain tile: Typically made from a dust-pressed method for a dense, fine grained finish.

Pre-finished: As in flooring, meaning that no other finishing is needed; only installation is required.

Primary Backing: *see* Backing

Q

Quarry tile: Using an extrusion process incorporating shale or clay, quarry tile is strong, thick and performs well. The most well known of the quarry tiles would be terra cotta.

Quarter sawn: Lumber is cut from a log at an angle of 45 to 90 degrees. An advantage to quarter sawn wood is that the board wears more evenly due to less twisting and cupping of the wood.

Quartz: A common mineral.

R

Random sheared: A level or high-low loop carpet or rug is lightly sheared so only the tops of the higher loops are affected. Whereas the uncut loops are brighter and reflect light better, the sheared areas pull back, offering a textured appearance.

Repeat: The distance from the center of one motif of a pattern to the center of the next.

Resilience: A flooring material that is able to recover its original appearance and thickness after being subjected to compression or crushing. The resilient category of flooring includes vinyl, rubber, cork and linoleum. Carpet also has resiliency capabilities within the recovery of its fibers after being trod upon.

Rift sawn: An expensive lumber cut compared to others, in which lumber is cut at 30 to 60 degree angles. There is more waste. Also known as a Bastard cut.

Rubber flooring: A resilient floor covering categorized by vibrant coloration and exceptional sound absorption. The rubber flooring of today also makes use of post industrial waste rubber and recycled auto tires, making it environmentally efficient.

S

Sandstone: A sedimentary rock composed of sand and quartz. Durable, with a high crushing and tensile strength, sandstone has a wide range of colors and textures.

Savonnerie: A hand-knotted rug, French made, pastel in hue, with a floral medallion set on an open field with stuttered borders.

Satin: A finish with a soft sheen.

Saxony: A cut pile carpet, Saxony offers a smooth nap. The extra twist in the yarn creates a dense, sophisticated blanket of fiber.

Sculptured: Referring to carpet and tile: High and low areas in a carpet, whether it is all loop or cut and loop; or high and low areas molded into the face of a piece of tile.

Secondary backing: *see* Backing

Seconds: Referring to imperfect, defective, or substandard products that have been rejected by a manufacturer as being subpar. Often, these products are sold at a deep discount. Depending upon the quality standards of any given manufacturer, a factory second may actually represent an excellent value.

Serging: In an area rug, serging would refer to a method of finishing the edges with a heavy yarn in a close stitch.

Shade: A color produced by adding black to a pigment. Can also be a change in an appearance of a rug or carpet due to the slant or tilt of fibers—a reflection of light.

Sisal: A natural plant fiber that can be woven, dyed or painted. Typically used as material for woven rugs and mats.

Slab: A lengthwise cut of a large quarry block of stone.

Slat: A small piece of hardwood that is used to form parquet squares.

Slate: A compact, metamorphic rock that can be split into slabs or plates. Embedded into cement or mortar, slate is a hard surfaced flooring.

Slip resistant: Small abrasive particles in the surface of stone or tile offer some resistance to slipping when trod upon. High gloss, smooth finishes are *less* slip resistant; matte finishes are *more* slip resistant.

Small-scale pattern: Patterns with small designs and smaller distances between repeats of that design.

Sprouting: When a carpet tuft or fiber rises up above the surface level. This may be alleviated by removing with scissors.

Stain resistant: (*also* Stain resistance, Soil resistant) The degree to which a floor covering can resist permanent discoloration and soiling. Most floor coverings have some type of chemical finish applied to inhibit exposure to stain and inhibit attachment of soil.

Sticking: Cementing together broken marble slabs or pieces.

Stretch: (*also* Stretch-in) An installation procedure in which residential carpet is pulled tautly over its cushion (pad) and onto tackless strips to secure it.

Strip flooring: A popular type of wood flooring no wider than 3¼" that are end matched and tongue and groove constructed. Installed in parallel rows, they are typically nailed down to the subfloor.

Subfloor: A rough, structural layer that provides support to the home's floor. It may have floor coverings installed directly upon it or may be the recipient of an underlayment. Typically lies on top of the floor's joists.

Surface layer: *see* Wear layer.

T

Tackless strip: A strip of metal or wood implanted with rows of tacks facing up and installed onto the floor. Carpet is then stretched and secured onto this strip to hold it in place.

Tensile strength: The amount of forced stretching a piece of fabric or yarn can accommodate before it breaks.

Terracotta: A type of tile, typically unglazed, offering variable color and water absorption. Used primarily indoors. Also known as "cotto."

Terrazzo: Marble or stone chips are embedded into cement and then highly polished until smooth. Traditionally created on the site, although sometimes premade tiles are available. Multicolored.

Tibetan rug: A rug produced in Tibet; some produced as early as the 1700s. Drew influence from China and Eastern Turkestan. Uses color and pattern to signify function. Hand-knotted, using a Tibetan technique resembling a continuous system of knots.

Tile: Typically, a ceramic piece usually made from clay or pressed dust. Can also include glass, porcelain and quarry. The sheer number of tile types is virtually uncatalogued. Can also be categorized as cultural, artistic, mosaic and stylistic.

Tint: A color produced when a pigment is mixed with white.

Tone on Tone: A pattern using two or more variations of the same hue to create depth and interest.

Tongue & Groove: Usually seen in any type of strip, plank or parquet flooring, in which there is a "tongue" on one side of each unit and a "groove" on the other end. The two are engaged together when matched end to end.

Beautiful wood floors need no introduction. Consider a lifetime of beauty by installing natural hardwood flooring.

Traffic: Referring to the amount of passing back and forth of humans and animals along the same path, such as how an entryway will receive more "traffic" than a spare bedroom, for example.

Travertine: A type of limestone that is a product of precipitation from ground water and around spring orifices.

Travertine marble: A limestone variety with a cellular structure concentrated in thin layers. Those layers that are able to take a high polish are classified as commercial marble.

Tufted carpet: A type of carpet manufactured by a tufting machine, in which tufts of yarn are inserted through a backing fabric, creating a pile of cut and/or loop ends. The most popular type of carpeting in North America.

Twist: The winding of a fiber around itself to strengthen its resistance to crushing. The tighter the twist, the more durable it will be.

U

Underlayment: (also underlay) A layer of material installed over the subfloor that provides a smooth, stable surface suitable to receive the floor covering. Can be cushion, plywood, foam pads, particle board and more depending upon the flooring selected. Also provides acoustical, wear and comfort benefits.

Urethane: A surface finish that holds its shine for a longer period of time than wax. Also resists stains more stringently than other finishes.

V

Veining: Intermittent natural colors occurring within stones such as marble, limestone and alabaster.

Veneer: A thin sheet of wood that has been sliced or sawed from a log. Usually applied over inferior wood or used as a décor surface.

Verde antique: Commercial marble (chiefly serpentine) that is able to take a high degree of polish. Commonly veined with calcite and dolomite.

Vinyl flooring: A resilient flooring material available in both sheet and tile, made from vinyl resins, plasticizers, pigments and other filler materials and additives. A wide variety of colors and patterns. Inexpensive.

W

Warp: When a piece of wood distorts from its true plane; in carpeting, it refers to yarn running lengthwise.

Warp yarn: *see* Warp

Waxing: Used in marble finishing: natural voids in marble are filled with color-blended material.

Wear layer: The top, surface layer of flooring, designed to protect the décor (beauty) layer.

Wear resistance: How well the wear layer reacts to foot traffic and other types of abuse.

Weft yarn: Yarn that runs the width of the carpet, as opposed to the length (warp) of the carpet.

White wood: Wood that has not been stained.

Wilton carpet: A woven carpet crafted in a wide variety of textures and patterns but with a narrow number of colors in each pattern.

Wood flooring: Available as solid wood, engineered or reclaimed, the most popular woods used today are oak, maple, birch, pecan and beech, although there are over fifty to choose from. Found primarily in plank and strips, wood flooring is a renewable and recyclable resource. A variety of grades, cuts and prefinishing options make wood flooring infinitely beautiful.

Wool: A natural animal fiber that captures dye well, and is soft and versatile.

Worm holes: Holes made by worms as they burr through trees.

Woven carpet: Lengthwise and widthwise yarns are woven together on a loom to form a fabric. Common names for woven carpets would be Axminster and Wilton, for example.

Y

Yarn: A continuous strand of fibers used in tufting and weaving to form carpet.

Yarn ply: The total quantity of single yarn threads twisted together to form a plied yarn.

Source Guide

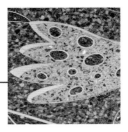

Beginning Pages

Cover: Capella Wood Floors, www.capellafloors.com, photograph by David Lyles; Inside front: Kirkstone, www.kirkstone.com; Title page: Integraf, Moscow, Russia; Copyright & contents pages: Oceanside Glasstile, www.glasstile.com; 6–7: Dal-Tile, www.daltile.com; 8–9: Forbo Linoleum, www.forbolinoleum na.com; 10: Robbins Fine Hardwood Flooring, www.armstrong.com; 11: Carina Works, Inc., www.carinaworks.com; 12: Florida Tile Industries, www.fltile.com; 13: Bronzework Studio/Lowitz & Co., www.lowitzandcompany.com, photo courtesy of Lowitz & Company

Hardwood

14–15: Osh-Kosh Floor Designs, www.oshkoshfloors.com, design by Eli Olivarez; 16: Photo courtesy of Goodwin Heart Pine, www.heartpine.com; 17: Duro Design, www.duro-design.com; 18: Photo courtesy of Aged Woods, www.agedwoods.com; 19 & 20: Goodwin Heart Pine, www.heartpine.com; 21 & 22: Pioneer Millworks, www.pioneermillworks.com; 23: Aged Woods, www.agedwoods.com, photo courtesy of Warren Jaeger Photography; 24: Hartco Quality Wood Flooring, www.armstrong.com; 25 (above): Boral Timber, www.boraltimber.com; 25 (below): Morelock Wood Products, www.morelockwood.com; 26–27: Anderson Hardwood Floors, www.andersonfloors.com; 28: Ekowood International/TSH Products, www.ekowood.com; 29:

Mohawk Industries, www.mohawkind.com; 30 (left): Duro Design, www.duro-design.com; 30 (above-right): Trestlewood, www.trestlewood.com; 31 (above right): Robbins Fine Hardwood Flooring, www.armstrong.com; 31 (right): Mohawk Industries, www.mohawkind.com; 32: Capella Wood Floors, www.capellafloors.com; 33: Osh-Kosh Floor Designs, www.oshkoshfloors.com; 34: Anderson Hardwood Floors, www.andersonfloors.com; 35: (above): Aged Woods, www.agedwoods.com; 35 (below): Morelock Wood Products, www.morelockwood.com; 36: Mohawk Industries, www.mohawkind.com; 37: (above-left): Osh-Kosh Floor Designs, www.oshkoshfloors.com; 37 (above-right): Boral Timber, www.boraltimber.com; 37 (below-left): Teragren LLC, www.teragren.com, photo courtesy of Teragren LLC; 37 (below-right): Integraf, Moscow, Russia; 38 (above): Bruce Hardwood Floors, www.armstrong.com; 38 (below): Par-ky, www.par-ky.com; 39: (above-left): Trestlewood, www.trestlewood.com; 39 (right): Morelock Wood Products, www.morelockwood.com; 40: Capella Wood Floors, www.capellafloors.com; 41: Capella Wood Floors, www.capellafloors.com, photo by David Lyles; 42 (above): Osk-Kosh Floor Designs, www.oshkoshfloors.com; 42 (below): Integraf, Moscow, Russia; 43 (above): Capella Wood Floors, www.capellafloors.com; 43 (below): Ekowood International/TSH Products, www.ekowood.com; 44: Ekowood International/TSH Products, www.ekowood.com; 45 (above): Teragren LLC, www.teragren.com, photograph by Steven

Young and courtesy of Teragren LLC; 45 (below): Hartco Quality Wood Flooring, www.armstrong.com; 46 (above): Capella Wood Floors, www.capellafloors.com; 46 (below): Parquet by Dian™, www.parquet.com; 47: Mohawk Industries, www.mohawkind.com; 48 (above): Goodwin Heart Pine, www.heartpine.com; 48 (below): Pioneer Millworks, www.pioneer-millworks.com; 49: Anderson Hardwood Floors, www.anderson-floors.com; 50: Capella Wood Floors, www.capella floors.com; 51 (above): Boral Timber, www.boraltimber.com; 51 (below): Integraf, Moscow, Russia, design by Valery Blinov & Tatiana Kotelnikova; 52 (above): Bruce Hardwood Floors, www.armstrong.com; 52 (left): Goodwin Heart Pine, www.heartpine.com; 53: Robbins Fine Hardwood Flooring, www.armstrong.com;54: Robbins Fine Hardwood Flooring, www.armstrong.com; 55 (above): Eterna Hardwood Flooring/Les Parquets Dubeau Ltd., www.parquetsdubeau.com; 55 (right): Anderson Hardwood Floors, www.andersonfloors.com

Carpet & Rugs

56–57: Central Oriental Floor Covering, www.centraloriental.com; 58: Oriental Weavers/ Sphinx, www.owarug.com, Andy Warhol®©The Andy Warhol Foundation; 59 & 60: Mohawk Industries, www.mohawkind.com; 61: Beaulieu of America, www.beaulieu-usa.com; 62 (left): Shaw Industries, www.shawfloors.com; 62 (right): Beaulieu of America, www.beaulieu-usa.com; 63 (left): Beaulieu of America,

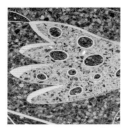

Source Guide

www.beaulieu-usa.com; 63 (right): Nourison USA, www.nourison.com; 64: Shaw Industries, www.shaw floors.com; 65: Godfrey Hirst USA Inc., www.godfreyhirst.com; 66: Mohawk Industries, www.mohawk ind.com; 67 (above): Bowron Sheepskin Co., www.bowron.com; 67 (below): Jaipur Rugs, Inc., www.jaipurrugs.com; 68–69: Central Oriental Floor Covering, www.cen-traloriental.com; 70: Odegard, www.odegardcarpets.com; 71: Tinnin Oriental, www.tinnen.com; 72 (left): Capel, Inc., www.capel-rugs.com; 72 (right): Odegard, www.odegardcarpets.com; 73: Oriental Weavers USA/Sphinx, www.owarug.com; 74 (below-left): Bowron Sheepskin Co., www.bowron.com; 74 (below-right): Oriental Weavers USA/ Sphinx, www.owarug.com; 75: Central Oriental Floor Covering, www.cen-traloriental.com; 76 (left): Beaulieu of America, www.beaulieu-usa.com; 76 (above): Oriental Weavers USA/Sphinx, www.owa rug.com; 77 (above): Shaw Industries, www.shawfloors.com; 77 (right): Mohawk Industries, www.mohawkind.com; 78 (left): Davis & Davis, www.davisrugs.com; 78 (right): Liora Manne, www.liora-manne.com; 79 (left): Odegard, www.odegard carpets.com; 79 (right): Central Oriental Floor Covering, www.centraloriental.com; 80: Beaulieu of America, www.beaulieu-usa.com; 81: Shaw Industries, www.shawfloors.com; 82 (left): Oriental Weavers USA/ Sphinx, www.owarug.com; 82 (cen-ter): Odegard, www.odegardcar-pets.com; 83: Liora Manne, www.lio-ramanne.com; 84 (above): Odegard, www.odegardcarpets.com; 84

(below): Shaw Industries, www.shawfloors.com; 85 (above): Shaw Industries, www.shawfloors .com; 85 (below): Oriental Weavers USA/Sphinx, www.owarug.com; 86 (left): Liora Manne, www.liora-manne.com; 86 (right): Central Oriental Floor Covering, www.cen-traloriental.com; 87 (left): Davis & Davis, www.davisrugs.com; 87 (right): Oriental Weavers USA /Sphinx, www.owarug.com

Resilient

88–89: Congoleum Corp., www.con-goleum.com; 90: AllState Rubber Corp., www.allstaterubber.com; 91 & 92: Armstrong World Industries, www.armstrong.com; 93: Amtico International Inc., www.amtico.com; 94: Polyflor, www.polyflor.com; 95: Armstrong World Industries, www.armstrong.com; 96 (above): Armstrong World Industries, www.armstrong.com; 96 (below): Congoleum Corp., www.con-goleum.com; 97 (above): Congoleum Corp., www.congoleum.com; 97 (below): Amtico International Inc., www.amtico.com; 98 & 99: Armstrong World Industries, www.armstrong.com; 100: Amtico International Inc., www.amtico.com; 101: Congoleum Corp., www.con-goleum.com; 102: (middle): Congoleum Corp., www.con-goleum.com; 103: Amtico International Inc., www.amtico.com; 104: Natural Cork, www.natural-cork.com; 105: Duro Design, www.duro-design.com; 106: Globus Cork, www.corkfloor.com; 107: Gerbert Limited, www.gerbertltd .com; 108: Natural Cork, www.nat-uralcork.com; 109 (above-left): Globus Cork, www.corkfloor.com; 109 (mid-dle, lower left and right): Expanko Cork, www.expanko.com; 110: Natural Cork, www.naturalcork .com; 111 & 112: Expanko Cork, www.expanko.com; 113 (above-left): Globus Cork, www.corkfloor.com; 113 (above-right): Dodge-Regupol, Inc., www.regupol.com; 113 (lower left): Duro Design, www.duro-design.com; 113 (lower right):

Expanko Cork, www.expanko.com; 114 (left): Duro Design, www.duro-design.com; 114 (above): Photograph courtesy of Expanko Cork, www.expanko.com; 115 (above): Photograph courtesy of Dodge-Regupol Inc., www.regupol .com; 115 (right): Duro Design, www.duro-design.com; 116: AllState Rubber Corp., www.allstaterubber .com; 117: Gerbert Limited, www.gerbertltd.com; 118: AllState Rubber Corp., www.allstaterubber .com; 119 (all photographs): Expanko Cork, www.expanko.com; 120: Armstrong World Industries, www.armstrong.com; 121, 122, 123 & 124 (both): Forbo Linoleum Inc., www.forbolinoleumna.com; 124 (left): Forbo Linoleum Inc., www.forbolinoleumna.com; 125 (both): Armstrong World Industries, www.armstrong.com; 126: Forbo Linoleum Inc., www.forbolinoleum-na.com; 126 (middle): Forbo Linoleum, www.forbolinoleumna .com; 127: Armstrong World Industries, www.armstrong.com; 128 (above left): Alloc Inc., www.alloc.com; 128 (middle left): Armstrong World Industries, www.armstrong.com

Laminate

128 (lower left): Quick-Step Flooring, www.quick-step.com; 128–129: inhaus Flooring, www.inhaus-style.com; 130: Pergo, www.pergo .com; 131: Alloc Inc., www.alloc .com; 132: Pergo, www.pergo.com; 133 (above): Alloc Inc., www.alloc .com; 133 (below): Quick-Step Flooring, www.quick-step.com; 134–135: inhaus Flooring, www.inhaus-style.com; 136 (above): Quick-Step Flooring, www.quick-step.com; 136 (below): Armstrong World Industries, www.armstrong .com; 137: Pergo, www.pergo.com; 138: inhaus Flooring, www.inhaus-style.com; 139 (above left): Abet Laminati, www.abetlaminati.com; 139 (middle left): Quick-Step Flooring, www.quick-step.com; 139 (lower left): Abet Laminati, www.abetlaminati.com; 139 (right):

Alloc Inc., www.alloc.com; 140 (above): Armstrong World Industries, www.armstrong.com; 140 (below): Alloc Inc., www.alloc.com; 141 (above): Armstrong World Industries, www.armstrong.com; 141 (below): Quick-Step Flooring, www.quick-step.com; 142 (above left): Abet Laminati, www.abetlaminati.com; 142 (middle left): inhaus Flooring, www.inhaus-style.com; 142 (lower left & right): Alloc Inc., www.alloc.com; 143 & 144: inhaus Flooring, www.inhaus-style.com; 145 (both): Alloc Inc., www.alloc .com; 146: inhaus Flooring, www.inhaus-style.com; 147: Armstrong World Industries, www.armstrong.com; 148 (above): Alloc Inc., www.alloc.com; 148 (below): Armstrong World Industries, www.armstrong.com; 149 (above): Mohawk Industries, www.mohawkind.com; 149 (below): inhaus Flooring, www.inhaus-style.com; 150: Armstrong World Industries, www.armstrong.com; 151: BHK of America, www.bhku-niclic.com; 152 (left): Mohawk Industries, www.mohawkind.com; 152 (above): BHK of America, www.bhkuniclic.com; 153 (above): inhaus Flooring, www.inhaus-style.com; 153 (right): Pergo, www.pergo.com; 154 (left): Armstrong World Industries, www.armstrong.com; 154 (right): Mohawk Industries, www.mohawk ind.com; 155 (left): Pergo, www.pergo.com; 155 (right): BHK of America, www.bhk uniclic.com; 156: Pergo, www.pergo.com; 157: BHK of America, www.bhkuniclic.com

Tile & Stone

158–159: Oceanside Glasstile, www.glasstile.com; 160: Armstrong World Industries, www.armstrong .com; 161: Epro Tile, www.epro tile.com; 162: Florida Tile Industries, www.fltile.com; 163 (above): Crossville Porcelain Stone/USA, www.crossville-ceramics.com; 163 (below): Dal-Tile Corp., www.daltile.com; 164–165: Bisazza

North America, www.bisazzausa .com, photo by Alberto Ferrero, project by Fabio Novembre; 166 (left): Oceanside Glasstile, www.glasstile .com, photo by Christopher Ray Photography; 166 (above): Kirkstone, www.kirkstone.com; 167 (above): Oceanside Glasstile, www.glasstile.com, photo by Christopher Ray Photography; 167 (below): Dal-Tile Corp., www.daltile.com; 168–169: Artistic Tile, www.artistictile.com photograph courtesy of Artistic Tile; 170: Kirkstone, www.kirkstone.com; 171 (above): Design by Teresa Cox, www.teresacox.com; 171 (below): Fritz Industries, www.fritztile.com; 172: Dal-Tile Corp., www.daltile.com; 173: Kiirkstone, www.kirkstone .com; 174: Artistic Tile, www.artistictile.com, photograph courtesy of Artistic Tile; 175: Kirkstone, www.kirkstone.com; 176 (left): Artistic Tile, www.artistictile.com, photograph courtesy of Artistic Tile; 176 (above): Kirkstone, www.kirkstone.com; 177 (above): Oceanside Glasstile, www.glasstile.com, photograph by Christopher Ray Photography; 177 (right): Design by Teresa Cox, www.teresacox.com; 178 (left): Florida Tile Industries, www.fltile.com; 178 (above): Ann Sacks, www.annsacks.com; 179 (above): Bisazza North America, www.bisazzausa .com, design by Carlo Del Bianco; 179 (right): Oceanside Glasstile, www.glasstile.com, photograph by Christopher Ray Photography; 180: (above): Armstrong World Industries, www.armstrong.com; 180 (right): Dal-Tile Corp., www.daltile .com; 181 (above): Crossville Porcelain Stone/USA, www.crossville-ceramics.com; 181 (below): Mohawk Industries, www.mohawkind.com; 182: Mohawk Industries, www.mohawk ind.com; 183: Florida Tile Industries, www.fltile.com; 184: Crossville Porcelain Stone/USA, www.crossville-ceramics.com; 184 (middle): Laufen Ceramic Tile Co., www.laufenusa.com; 185: Dal-Tile Corp., www.daltile.com; 186

(above): Bisazza North America, www.bisazzausa.com, photograph by Alberto Ferrero, Fabio Novembre, architect; 186 (below): Armstrong World Industries, www.armstrong.com; 187 (above): Armstrong World Industries, www.armstrong.com; 187 (below): Laufen Ceramic Tile Co., www.laufenusa.com; 188 (left): Dal-Tile Corp., www.daltile.com; 188 (above): Design by Dahli deLeon-Brant, Capital Designs West, 310/395-2053; 189 (above): Artistic Tile, www.artistictile.com, photograph courtesy of Artistic Tile; 189 (right): Dal-Tile Corp., www.daltile.com; 190 (above): Kirkstone, www.kirkstone.com; 190 (right): Design by Dahli deLeon-Brant, Capital Designs West, 310/395-2053, photograph courtesy of Steve Gunther; 190 (above): Artistic Tile, www.artistictile.com, photograph courtesy of Artistic Tile; 191 (above): Artistic Tile, www.artistictile.com, photograph courtesy of Artistic Tile; 191 (below): Armstrong World Industries, www.armstrong .com; 192: Dal-Tile Corp., www.daltile .com; 193: Kirkstone, www.kirkstone.com; 194 (left): Kirkstone, www,kirkstone.com; 196 (above): Fritz Industries, www.fritztile.com; 196 (below): Ann Sacks, www.annsacks.com; 197 (above): Dal-Tile Corp., www.daltile .com; 197 (below): Kirkstone, www.kirkstone .com; 198 (left): Armstrong World Industries, www.armstrong .com; 198 (above): Crossville Porcelain Stone/USA, www.crossville-ceramics.com; 199 (both): Crossville Porcelain Stone/USA, www.crossville-ceram-ics.com; 200: (left): Artistic Tile, www.artistictile .com, photograph

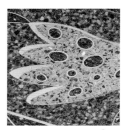

Source Guide

courtesy of Artistic Tile; 200 (right): Dal-Tile Corp., www.daltile.com; 201 (left & right):, 202: Florida Tile Industries, www.fltile.com; 203: Laufen Ceramic Tile Co., www.laufenusa .com; 204 (left): Island Stone, www.islandstoneusa .com; 204 (above): Bronzework Studios/ Lowitz & Co., www.lowitzandcompany.com, photograph courtesy of Lowitz and Company; 205 (above): Bronzework Studios/Lowitz & Co., www.lowitzandcompany.com, photograph courtesy of Lowitz and Company; 205 (right): Dal-Tile Corp., www.daltile.com; 206 (left): Oceanside Glasstile, www.glasstile.com; 206 (middle): Crossville Porcelain Stone/USA, www.crossville-ceramics.com; 207: Florida Tile Industries, www.fltile.com; 208 (left): Laufen Ceramic Tile Co., www.laufenusa .com; 208 (above): Metropolitan Ceramics, www.metroceramics.com; 209: Mohawk Industries, www.mohawkind.com 210–211: Artistic Tile/Casa Domani, www.artistictile.com, photograph

Alternative Floor Coverings

courtesy of Artistic Tile; 212: Arcon International, www.arconinternational.com, design by Dahli deLeon-Brant, Capital Designs West, 310/395-2053, photograoh courtesy of Steve Gunther; 213: Design by Wendy Richens, Richens Designs Inc., 310/385-8450; 214: Historic Floorcloths, www.stores.ebay .com/historicfloorcloths; 215 (above): Bronzework Studios/ Lowitz & Co., www.lowitzandcompany.com, photograph courtesy of

Lowitz and Company; 215 (below): Carina Works, Inc., www.carinaworks.com; 216 (left): Carina Works, www.carinaworks.com; 216 (middle): Historic Floorcloths, www.stores.ebay.com/historicfloorcloths; 217: Carina Works, www.carinaworks.com; 218 (above): Bronzework Studios/Lowitz & Co., www.lowitzandcompany.com, photograph courtesy of Lowitz and Company; 218 (below): Carina Works, www.carinaworks.com; 219 (above): Bronzework Studios/ Lowitz & Co., www.lowitzandcompany.com, photograph courtesy of Lowitz and Company; 219 (below): Design by Sylvia Beez, M.A.P. Interiors, www.mapinteriors.com; 220: Artistic Tile/Casa Domani, www.artistictile .com, design by Edward R. Stough, ASID, www.edwardrstough.com, photograph by Ron Solomon; 221: Durafloor, www.durafloor.com; 222: Amtico International, www.amtico .com

Misc. End Pages

228: Forbo Linoleum, www.forbolinoleum na.com; 231: Anderson Hardwood Floors, www.andersonfloors.com; 233–236: Terrazzo detail by Teresa Cox, www.teresacox.com; 237–239: Ann Sacks, www.annsacks.com; 240: Liora Manne, www.lioramanne.com; Back cover: (first, second, third): Amtico International, Inc., www.amtico.com; (fourth): Capella Wood Floors, www.capellafloors.com; (fifth): Nourison USA, www.nourison.com

Index

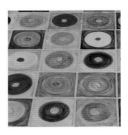

A

Above grade: 223
Acclimation: 223
Acid-Stained (washed): 212
Acrylic: 62, 108
Acrylic impregnated: 26
Adhesive: 223
Allergies: 123
Alpine ash: 25
Aluminum oxide: 101
Ambering: 124, 223
Ash: 26, 55
Aubusson: 68

B

Back layer: 131
Bamboo: 17, 26, 30–31, 45, 96, 203
Basaltina: 194
Basketweave: 169, 219, 224
Beech: 29, 39, 50, 157
Below grade: 224
Berber: 59, 62, 65, 81, 224
Birch: 10, 37, 42, 50, 53, 152
Bloodwood: 47
Braided: 68, 224
Brass: 33
Brazil nut: 138
Brick: 169, 208, 211, 213, 216
Broadloom: 61, 85, 224
Brocade: 68
Bronze: 205, 207, 214–215

C

Calcite: 174
Carpet(ing): 6, 8–9, 11, 16, 57–87, 162
Carpet backing: 224

Ceramic: 12, 28, 159–160, 162, 164, 183, 193, 224
Cherry: 15, 37, 41–42, 49, 53, 137, 139
Chestnut: 18, 23
Clay: 160–161, 164, 208
Cleft(ed): 159, 171, 183, 189–191
Cobblestone: 169
Coir: 62
Concrete: 102, 207, 211–212, 219, 221, 224
Cork: 89–91, 104, 106–109, 111–112, 114–115, 120, 224
Cotton: 68, 70
Cradle-to-cradle: 89
Cupping: 43
Cut and Loop Pile: 65, 225
Cut Pile Loop: 65, 225
Cypress: 18, 49

D

Décor (beauty) layer: 131, 134, 138, 225
Direct laminate: 131, 225
Dhurrie: 68, 225
Drugget: 68, 225

E

Emboss(ed): 68, 187, 225
Embossed-in-register: 130, 134, 138, 145, 225
Engineered wood: 15, 26, 41, 45, 47, 50, 53, 55, 225
Engrave: 68
Environmentally-conscious (friendly, responsible): 9, 39, 45, 47, 63, 75, 89–90, 104, 120, 123, 228
Environmental effects: 20, 24, 62, 124
Exotic: 17, 24, 26, 29, 39, 170
Extrude(d): 159, 164

F

Faux: 11, 215, 219
Feldspar: 174–175
Fiber: 62–63, 65, 68, 79, 82
Fiberboard: 131
Field tile: 159, 163, 178, 184, 188–189, 203, 205, 225
Flagstone: 169, 226
Flamed: 159, 169
Flax: 62, 124
Floating floor: 28, 104, 129, 226
Floorcloth: 214, 216–217
Frieze: 61, 65, 226
Fur: 68, 226

G

Gabbeh: 68, 226
Glass tile: 159, 162, 164, 166, 186, 194, 226
Glaze(d): 11, 159, 161–162, 164, 167, 181, 184, 187–188, 191, 194, 198–199, 208, 226
Glueless locking system (technology): 24, 104, 129, 141, 155, 157
Grade: 29–30, 32, 43, 226
Grain: 18, 33, 35, 37, 136, 149, 153, 157, 174
Granite: 169–170, 174–175, 196, 226
Green design: 9
Grout: 140, 145, 153, 161–162, 205, 226
Growth ring: 17, 226

Index

H

Hand: 70, 226
Hand-hooked (tufted): 68, 72, 87, 226
Hand-knotted: 67–68, 70–71, 226
Hand-scraped: 16, 26, 49
Hand-woven: 70
Hardwood: 6, 8, 10, 15–55, 66, 108, 134, 149, 226, 231
Heart pine: 18, 21, 30, 49
Heartwood: 18, 21, 53
Herringbone: 191
High pressure laminate: 131, 226
Honed: 169, 174, 176, 187, 193–194, 196
Humidity: 20, 24, 32, 106, 134

I

Igneous: 174
Inlay: 15, 28, 33, 49. 126
Insulation: 60
Ipe: 33

J

Jarrah: 29
Jute: 62, 227

K

Karri: 37
Kilim: 66, 70, 227
Knot(s): 33, 70, 143, 227
Knot count: 70

L

Lacewood: 33
Laminate: 9, 128–157, 227
Lamontage: 78, 82
Leather: 28, 211, 213, 221
Level loop pile: 65, 227
Limestone: 102, 173–174, 180, 188, 193–194, 196, 215, 218, 227
Linoleum: 8, 11, 16, 89–91, 120–126, 227–228
Listello: 178, 183
Longstrip: 29

M

Mahal: 70, 227
Maintenance: 10–11, 63, 119, 152, 201
Maple: 26, 29, 31, 37, 42, 45, 47, 55, 95, 136, 149
Marble: 164, 169, 171, 174–175, 183, 189, 196, 198, 201, 219, 227
Matte: 164, 187, 227
Medallion: 70, 175, 196
Metal: 28, 211, 214–215, 217–218
Merbau: 26, 142
Metamorphic: 174–175
Mica: 174
Mildew: 60, 106
Moisture: 9, 20, 24, 60, 79, 106, 131, 146, 152, 154–155, 162, 164, 198, 214
Mold: 60, 106
Mosaic: 109, 112, 164, 169, 173–174, 178–179, 181, 186, 188, 193, 196, 215, 219, 227
Multi loop pile: 65, 227

N

Needlepoint: 70
Nylon: 58, 61–62, 75–77, 81, 86, 101

O

Oak: 16, 26, 29, 31, 37, 39, 50, 55, 98, 129, 131, 146, 153
Olefin: 62
Onyx: 175
Oriental rug: 70–71, 79, 227

P

Painted rug: 70, 214, 229
Parquet: 28, 42, 50, 229
Pattern: 9
Pear wood: 50
Pebble: 169
Pecan: 25–26, 33, 43, 53, 151
Persian rug: 70, 229
Pickled: 229
Pile: 57, 68, 75, 79, 229
Pileless: 70
Pill: 86, 229
Plainsawn: 31, 229
Plank: 31–33, 35, 37, 41, 47, 50, 53, 55, 98, 104, 129–130, 133–134, 139, 141–143, 146, 154, 190, 218, 229
Plush: 65, 84, 229
Ply: 229
Poly-vinyl Chloride (PVC): 90, 92, 118
Polypropylene: 62, 72, 75, 82, 86
Polyurethane: 107, 109
Poplar: 15
Porcelain: 11–12, 159, 161–164, 180–181, 183–184, 187–188, 191, 193–194, 196, 198, 200, 203, 207, 229
Power loom: 72, 75, 85
Pre-finished: 229
Pricing: 11

Q

Quarry: 102, 159, 164, 208, 229
Quartersawn: 31, 42, 50, 229
Quartz: 95, 174–175, 229

R

Radiant heat: 12–13, 26, 162
Rag rug: 70
Random sheared: 229
Reclaimed wood: 15, 18, 20, 26,
Recycle(d): 18, 116
Red oak: 26,
Redwood: 18
Refinishing: 17
Renewable resource: 104
Resilient flooring: 6, 11, 16, 88–127,
   162, 170, 229
Resistance (fire/scratch/slip/soil/
   stain/water): 9, 60, 66, 75, 92, 94
   101–102, 129, 132, 155, 162–164,
   181, 207, 225, 230
Riftsawn: 31, 229
River recovered (reclaimed): 18, 30,
   49, 53
Rubber flooring: 89–91, 116–119,
   229
Rug: 9, 57–87

S

Safety: 9, 95
Sandblasted: 169
Sanding(ed): 17, 20, 24, 26, 32, 132
Sandstone: 175, 204, 229
Satin: 229
Satinwood: 47
Savonnerie: 70, 229
Saw-cut: 169
Saxony: 65, 230
Sedimentary: 174–175
Shag carpet: 16, 65
Shale: 161, 164, 208
Sheepskin: 67–68
Sheet: 89, 92, 94–98, 101–102, 104
Silk: 62, 70, 82
Sisal: 62, 230
Slab: 169–170, 190, 230
Slate: 11, 89, 92, 96, 153, 171, 173,
   183, 189–191, 194, 197–198, 200,
   205, 207, 230

Solid wood: 15,
Sprouting: 230
Stain protection: 9
Stone: 11, 35, 120, 131–132, 145,
   158–209
Strip flooring: 32, 43, 45, 135, 151,
   230
Subfloor: 8, 28, 170, 230
Surface layer: 230
Sustainable harvest: 53
Synthetic: 58, 116

T

Tapestry: 67
Teak: 39, 43
Terracotta: 164, 190, 230
Terrazzo: 171, 175, 177, 196, 230
Tibetan rug: 70, 230
Tile: 12, 28, 90–92, 94, 97, 101–102,
   104, 111–112, 119, 123, 132, 134,
   140, 145, 151, 153, 158–209,
   213–214, 217–219, 230
Tongue & groove: 230
Traffic area: 203, 232
Travertine: 140, 175, 201, 215, 232
Tuft(ing/ed): 58, 232
Tumbled: 159, 189, 193

U

Underlayment: 28, 131, 134, 152, 232
Urethane: 92, 104, 109, 112, 232

V

V-groove: 133, 142
Veneer(ed): 39, 134, 232
Vinyl: 6, 16, 28, 60, 89, 91, 96–98,
   101–102, 124, 222, 232
Viscose: 62

W

Walnut: 26, 37, 42, 45, 47, 50, 149,
   190

Index

Warhol, Andy: 58, 76
Warp: 13, 232
Wear layer (surface, system): 26, 41,
   232
Wear resistant: 86, 232
Wear through: 157
Weave: 70
Wenge: 15, 42
White oak: 15, 23
Wood: 8, 11, 15, 60, 130–134, 136,
   139, 142, 152–153, 161, 231, 232
Wool: 57–58, 62–63, 67–68, 70–72, 78,
   82, 84, 86–87, 232
Wormholes: 232

Y

Yarn: 59, 63, 65, 67–68, 86, 232
Yellowheart: 33, 131

Resources

The following books and websites were used as resources in compiling this book:

Books:

Bukowski, Steven, *Flooring Instant Answers*, McGraw-Hill, Companies, Inc., USA, 2003

de Moubray, Amicia and David Black, *Carpets for the Home*, Rizzoli International Publications, Inc., New York, New York, 1999.

Editors of Sunset Books, *Ideas for Great Floors*, Sunset Books, Menlo Park, California, 2002.

Herbers, Jill, with photographs by Roy Wright, *Tile*, Artisan, A Division of Workman Publishing, Inc., New York, New York, 996.

Herbert, Tony and Kathryn Huggins, *The Decorative Tile in Architecture and Interiors*, Phaidon Press Limited, London, England, 1995.

Jones, Owen, *The Grammar of Ornament, A Unique Collection of More than 2,350 Classic Patterns*, DK Publishing, Inc., New York, New York, 2001; first published in 1856 by Day and Son, Lincoln's Inn Felds, London.

Jones, Sheila, *Resilient Flooring: A Comparison of Vinyl, Linoleum and Cork*, Georgia Tech Research Institute, 1999. (Technical paper)

Miller, Judith, *Influential Styles, From Baroque to Bauhaus—Inspiration for Today's Interiors*, Watson-Guptill Publications, New York, NY, 2003.

Mostaedi, Arian, *The American House Today-Architecture Showcase*, Carles Broto i Comerma, Barcelona, Spain, 2002

Powell, Jane with photographs by Linda Svendsen, *Linoleum*, Gibbs Smith, Layton, Utah, 2003.

Susanka, Susan, *Creating the Not So Big House, Insights and Ideas for the New American Home*, The Taunton Press, Newton, CT, 2000

Woloszynska, Suzanne, *The Art of Interior Design—Selecting Elements for Distinctive Styles*, Creative Publishing International, Inc., Minneapolis, MN, 2000

Websites

www.bobvila.com
www.carpet-rug.com
www.csmonitor.com/2004/0518/p18s02-hfks.html
www.flooringfacts.com
www.flooringguide.com
www.infotile.com
www.nafcd.org
www.nalfa.com
www.tileusa.com
www.Washingtonian.com
www.wfca.org
www.woodfloors.org

Please also refer to the Source Guide for individual website listings for each company featured in this book. Each site will offer valuable information on the products shown.